MW01491748

TWO PATHS

Papal Monarchy - Collegial Tradition

Rome's Claims of Papal Supremacy in the Light of the Orthodox Church

To

Marguerite

for her boundless love and loyalty

TWO PATHS

Papal Monarchy - Collegial Tradition

Rome's Claims of Papal Supremacy in the Light of the Orthodox Church

Michael Whelton

1998

© Michael Whelton, 1998

ISBN 0-9649141-5-8

All Scriptural quotations are from the Douay-Rheims version unless otherwise noted.

Regina Orthodox Press

PO Box 5288 Salisbury MA 01952

800 636 2470

Non US 978 462 7645 FAX 978 462 5079

Order over the WEB!

www.reginaorthodoxpress.com

CONTENTS

ADVANCE PRAISE FOR TWO PATHS

'Two Paths' is a historical record of the Roman Catholic claim regarding papal primacy and infallibility. As a member of the Orthodox Christian Church under the Patriarchate of Constantinople, I must admit that I am truly saddened by the efforts taken by the Roman Catholic Church to cast aside the importance of history, tradition and even the New Testament in order to sustain a teaching that has no basis in these three areas. I am disturbed because history is important to God Himself Who entered it, so that mankind might have the opportunity of knowing the creator.
I am convinced that much of the information in 'Two Paths' is unknown to most people. Roman Catholics and Orthodox Christians alike, who may have dreamed of reunion of the two churches will awaken to reality when they read this book.
I encourage all who believe in One, Holy, Catholic and Apostolic church to read 'Two Paths.' It is not easily put aside once one begins to read it. I am truly impressed by the historic documentation which it contains. It is a must read book.

Metropolitan ISAIAH + Greek Orthodox Diocese of Denver.

An ardent, thorough examination of the devolution of Rome's legitimate 'primacy of honor' in the ancient Christian Church into the ill-founded, problematic, and divisive doctrine of papal infallibility in the 19th century and its modern repercussions.
Although humbly offered as the result of personal research by an ex-Catholic convert to Orthodoxy, this cogent volume nevertheless synthesize the welter of important evidence on the issue of papal authority, and newly problematizes both the liturgical reforms of Vatican II and the current discussions of a reunion of the Western and Eastern branches of Christendom. It will surely-and ought to-provoke a Roman Catholic response, perhaps inaugurating a more informed discussion of the theological legitimacy of Roman claims to ecclesiastical supremacy in contradistinction to the conciliar model retained in the East.

Kimberley Patton, Assistant Professor in the Comparative
and Historical Study of Religion,
Harvard Divinity School.

About the Author

Michael Whelton was born in the United Kingdom where, having completed high school, he moved to Canada and studied for two years at York University in Toronto. After a stint as a job and wage analyst at the Canadian Broadcasting Corporation in Toronto, Ontario, he moved his young family to Southern California. The next seven years were spent as a stockbroker with two New York Stock Exchange member firms in the Los Angeles area, where he conducted numerous investment seminars and made guest appearances on Los Angeles public television.

After returning to Canada, Michael formed his own consulting company, in the Vancouver area of British Columbia. For the last ten years he has lived on a fifteen-acre hobby farm in the lush farm country of south west British Columbia with Marguerite, his wife of thirty seven years and three of their seven children. On Lazarus Saturday, 1995, Michael entered the Orthodox Church with Marguerite and one of their daughters. Their eldest daughter, her husband and their four children later joined them.

Michael and Marguerite have been very involved with the Pro-Life movement for the past twenty-three years. This commitment has entailed Michael serving as a Pro-Life director on two separate hospital boards, for a total of six years in the greater Vancouver area. The writing of Two Paths was the result of a long spiritual journey for the true Church and was greatly aided by a life long interest in history.

Acknowledgements

Without the help and support of my wife Marguerite, this book would never have seen the light of day. Her typing, editing and endless proof reading were invaluable.

A deep debt of gratitude also goes to our daughter Karen and her husband Benjamin for their help and encouragement. Benjamin is especially remembered for cheerfully responding to our numerous appeals for his computer expertise.

CHAPTER I

An Insistent Call

The years following the Second Vatican Council 1963-1965, were years of tremendous upheaval in the church for Roman Catholics. When all the changes were made to the mass in 1968, my wife and I like many Roman Catholics at the time, were uneasy with some of these innovations. Mass in the vernacular we thought was a good idea, however; the priest celebrating mass facing the people seemed like a major departure from liturgical tradition turning the priest into a sort of "master of ceremonies", while we found the new prayers dull and pedestrian, lacking the poetical quality of the older ones.

By the mid-nineteen-seventies, it was obvious that something had gone terribly wrong. Defections both lay and clerical were increasing in alarming numbers; for example, during the thirty years following the Council, 1965-1995 some twenty five million Roman Catholics had left the Church in North America alone; while hundreds of thousands of religious world-wide had abandoned their vocations. The cause of this debacle I believe (which is a belief shared by many), is the new mass which Pope Paul VI foisted on the church in 1968.

Christianity is a liturgical religion i.e., the very centre of our spiritual lives is the liturgical celebration of the Eucharist. As with any religious worship an implicit theology is always reflected in prayers, incense, gestures, music, dress and in style of architecture. Dramatically change this and you will change the faith. This is a truth reflected in the ancient law of the Church - lex orandi, lex credendi - the law of prayer is the law of belief. In his book, *Histoire des Variations des Eglises Protestants,* Catholic historian Bishop Bossuet describes how liturgical experimentation denied Protestants doctrinal cohesion; shattering them into numberless different denominations. Thomas Cranmer, Archbishop of Canterbury under Henry VIII understood this very well when he destroyed the Roman Catholic Church in England by changing the liturgy. Many of the changes he introduced are frighteningly similar to the new mass, as brilliantly analyzed by Catholic author Michael Davies in his book, *Cranmer's Godly Order.*[1]

Most Roman Catholics do not read Papal Encyclicals or Papal Addresses; the Church speaks to her faithful as she always has, through the liturgy. Thus Rome's foremost liturgical scholar, Monsignor Klaus Gamber, explains in his book, *Reform of the Roman Liturgy,*[2] (warmly endorsed by Cardinal Ratzinger, Prefect of the Congregation for the Faith) that liturgy and faith are interwoven and together form a fabric of belief. The old mass that reflected the traditional truths of the faith in its rubrics and piety, had been suppressed. In its place, as a concession to the ecumenical movement, we were given a new rite with scripture readings that pointedly eliminated any passages that warned us that while we

---

1 Cranmers Godly Order - Michael Davies, Devon 1976.

2 The Reform of the Roman Liturgy - page 100, Monsignor Klaus Gamber, Una Voce Press, San Juan Capistrano, California and Foundation for Catholic Reform, Harrison, New York, 1993.

have a loving God, He is also a God who will judge us. In the same vein the traditional prayers and hymns that once reminded us in majestic prose and lyrics, that we have a soul which we could lose, have been replaced with new ones that, lacking any reference to our eternal outcome, are vapid and vacuous.

Monsignor Gamber[3] also claims that the new liturgical rite has diluted the sacrificial aspect of the mass and has reduced mystical and dramatic ritual to an absolute minimum - just enough, no more - to ensure validity. Particularly scandalous for him, was changing the words Pro Multus (for many) by Paul VI, uttered by Christ at the Last Supper, to "For All", during the consecration - a crass concession to modern theology. On the wider implications of the new liturgical rite, Monsignor Gamber has this to say:

> ...the liturgical reform welcomed with so much idealism and hope by many priests and lay people alike has turned out to be a liturgical destruction of startling proportions - a debacle worsening with each passing year. Instead of the hoped-for renewal of the Church and of Catholic life, we are now witnessing a dismantling of the traditional values and piety on which our faith rests. Instead of a fruitful renewal of the liturgy, what we see is the destruction of the forms of the Mass which had developed organically during the course of many centuries.

---

3 Ibid., - page 12.

> Added to this state of affairs, is the shocking assimilation of Protestant ideas brought into the Church under the guise of the misunderstood term ecumenism, with a resulting growing estrangement from the ancient Churches of the East, that is, a turning away from the common tradition that has been shared by the East and the West up to this point in our history.[4]

The Protestant ideas which so shocked Monsignor Gamber had their origins in the highest authority of the Roman Catholic Church - the then reigning pontiff Pope Paul VI as Gamber points out:

> Neither the persistent entreaties of distinguished cardinals, nor serious dogmatic points raised about the new liturgy, nor urgent appeals from around the world not to make the new Missal mandatory could stop Pope Paul VI - a clear indication of his own, strong personal endorsement. Even the threat of a new schism - the Lefevre case - could not move him to have the traditional ritus Romanus at least coexist with the new rite - a simple gesture of pluralism and inclusiveness, which, in our day and age, certainly would have been a politic thing to do.[5]

This view was made clear in a nationally broadcasted radio programme ,"Ici Lumiere 101" in France on December 13, 1993. The guests were, Eyves Chiron, author of the book *Paul VI, le pape ecartele* and Jean Guitton, a member of the French Academy, author

---

4 Ibid., - page 9.
5 Ibid., - page 45.

and close friend of Paul VI. During the radio interview the following conversation took place:

> GUITTON:.....but I can only repeat that Paul VI did all that he could to bring the Catholic Mass away from the tradition of the Council of Trent towards the Protestants Lord's Supper...... In other words, we see in Paul VI an ecumenical intention to wipe out or at least to correct or soften everything that is too Catholic in the Mass and to bring the Catholic Mass, again I say, as close as possible to the Calvinist liturgy.
>
> CHIRON: Clearly that is a revolution in the Church.
>
> GUITTON; Clearly so.[6]

Some years ago, when we were living in California, we watched a movie called *Catholics* written by Brian Moore a lapsed Irish Catholic. This prophetic story concerns a monastery in Southern Ireland that continues to celebrate the Old Mass of the Tridentine Rite in defiance of the Vatican and the World Ecumen Council and since this is the only place left in the world that still celebrates the Old Mass, it is an international pilgrimage centre. The Vatican sends a young priest named Fr. Kinsella, played by Martin Sheen, to close them down. As a practicing Roman Catholic at the time, this movie really depressed me for the simple reason that there was more than a grain of truth in it.

---

6 The Latin Mass - Volume 4, Number l, Winter 1995, Foundation for Catholic Reform, Fort Collins, Colorado.

CHAPTER I

Artists like Brian Moore understand very well the importance of symbolism in ritual. In her book *The Desolate City*, Anne Roche Muggeridge discusses this Irish playwright and his prophetic novel *Catholics* in which he dealt with the destruction of the old Mass:

> Brian Moore is a lapsed Catholic but his instructive imagination remembers what it all meant and he has the great artists understanding of symbol. Explaining why he wrote "Catholics", he offered the inimitably Irish explanation that after a long absence he went to Mass and found that the thing he had stopped believing in was no longer there.[7]

As the years rolled by, the liturgical innovations increased as foretold by Monsignor Gamber making the traditional church a more distant image; a mirage that was more rapidly receding beyond our reach and as traditional Roman Catholics we became more and more like orphans in our church. One of the problems with the Mass is that it is seen as the, 'fruit of development' as opposed to the Orthodox which according to Cardinal Ratzinger: 'does not see liturgy as developing or growing in history, but only the reflection of the eternal liturgy, whose light, through the sacred celebration, illumines our changing times with its unchanging beauty and grandeur'.[8] The only consolation we received from the few traditional priests we knew was, "stick with the Pope, the Church has been through this before".

---

7 The Desolate City - page 134, Anne Roche Muggeridge, McClelland & Stuart Limited,. Toronto, 1986.

8 The Latin Mass, Vol. 2, No. 1, page 21, Jan/Feb. 1993.

However, the defections and loss of faith both in Europe and North America was unprecedented and the very institutions for transmitting the faith i.e. schools, colleges, universities and seminaries were collapsing.

Our spiritual journey to Orthodoxy began in 1992, when my wife took a course in Iconography from a Russian icon master in Vancouver, British Columbia. The icon is not only a window to the spiritual world, but is also a reflection of the traditions of the Orthodox Church. It is interesting that iconographic art always struck us as a more mature religious art form and that partly explains why we always had icons in our home. During this time we also attended some lectures on iconography organized by the Orthodox Church and were impressed by the humility, kindness and depth of spirituality of those present.

In 1993 we attended Easter Mass at our local parish church where, as with most Catholic churches today, the usual Protestant influence was very present. There were the familiar felt banners hanging in and around the sanctuary and the guitar group was belting those dreadful songs from the Glory and Praise Hymn Book. Musical instruments were thoroughly condemned by the Church Fathers[9] and whenever I heard those twanging guitars, I would inwardly genuflect to their wisdom. Yes, as with many traditional Catholics, we were receiving our weekly dose of what psychologists call cognitive dissonance, i.e. a feeling of alienation from the church's liturgy.

---

9 Encyclopaedia Britannica, Vol. no. 15, page 1065, 1972.

CHAPTER I

On our way home from mass, we visited a small Orthodox Church which had recently taken over the premises from a disused Protestant Church. Most of the parishioners were English speaking converts. A small untrained choir chanted the liturgy and some icons hung from a makeshift iconostasis - the difference was stunning - in these somewhat meager surroundings, they had captured a sense of transcendence, reverence, mystery and a vibrancy that we had lost. Despite our admiration for their liturgy, there was also a reaction to the unfamiliar - a feeling of alienation that would be more strongly felt when we visited the ethnic Orthodox Churches. We had always been aware of the Orthodox Church and her splendid witness to tradition, but today in this little bare bones church, the difference was especially striking and the questions started to gnaw at us. Why have they been able to maintain what we have lost? Some of the initial questions were typically those coming from Roman Catholics. How can they do this with a form of church government that is so decentralized? How can they manage their church organization without an authority figure like that of the Pope? Who is in charge? We contacted several Orthodox priests with whom we had many discussions and they were very helpful in steering us towards some Orthodox historians. Being keen students of history, we had read about the Early Church but mostly from a Catholic point of view. Here for the first time we were reading books where the Orthodox Church was speaking for herself. As most people know, both Roman Catholic and Orthodox Churches were one church for the first thousand years. It should be pointed out that the

Orthodox Church during those first thousand years of union, always recognized Rome as having a Primacy of Honour i.e. primus inter pares - first among equals. It was the ancient seat of Roman government and was the resting-place of Peter and Paul which for many hundreds of years proved to be a steadfast witness to the true faith. The Orthodox Church believes that Rome erred in attempting to turn this Primacy of Honour within the Church to a Supremacy over the Church. Reading these Orthodox scholars was like having a long lost relative showing up on your doorstep and filling in details of family history, thereby offering a fresh perspective.

This new perspective challenged our most deeply held beliefs concerning the Papacy and the development of the early church. Like most Roman Catholics, we took the triumphant, monarchical Papacy of the high middle ages like that of Gregory VII, Innocent III and Boniface VIII and attempted to carry this concept of the Papacy back to the very early church. Like most Roman Catholics our view of the Church was more picturesque than real.

For non-Roman Catholics, it is almost impossible to comprehend the attachment a Catholic has for the Papacy and our reaction was highly defensive. In the past, when we came across serious works of history which contradicted the Roman Catholic position, we were skeptical and if we found that the author was Protestant, or the book came from a Protestant publishing house, it was given scant attention and if it contradicted a dogmatic belief it was dismissed immediately. Only Roman Catholic historians have a pure line to objectivity, especially when it concerns articles of faith. This is what Catholics are taught and it is this belief that will keep their faith inviolate. This teaching is best exemplified by Pope Leo XIII in his celebrated *Letter to the Prelates and Clergy of France* (September 8th, 1899). While encouraging them to the study of history he reminds "Those who study it must never lose sight of the fact that it contains a collection of dogmatic facts, which impose themselves upon our faith, and which nobody is ever permitted to call in doubt". Cardinal Manning of England is even more blunt, "The appeal to antiquity is both a treason and a heresy. It is a treason because it rejects the divine voice of the Church at this hour, and a heresy because it denies that voice to be divine".[10] At another time Cardinal Manning wrote, "The appeal from the living voice of the Church to any tribunal whatsoever, human history included is an act of private judgment and a treason because that living voice is supreme; and to appeal from that supreme voice is also a heresy because that voice by divine assistance is infallible."[11]

Thus for Catholics, that the Bishops of Rome have always exercised immediate and supreme jurisdiction and infallible judgment over the entire church and that these prerogatives were transmitted by Peter, is a dogmatic belief beyond dispute. However, we took the momentous step to allow our position to be challenged to close scrutiny thus, we sought out good, competent non-Catholic, non-Orthodox scholars and spent the next

---

10 Temporal Mission of the Holy Ghost, 4th Edition, page 238.

11 Daily Telegraph, 8th, October 1875, page 5.

two years reading all aspects of church history, contacting distant libraries and Universities, verifying quotes, translating Latin documents and holding discussions with several Roman Catholic priests. What we found was that contemporary scholarship and early church writings confirmed the Orthodox position. We have always striven to confront difficulties without prejudice and problems without sentiment and these values were sorely tested when we looked at the Orthodox Church. There were times when we were praying for a good argument to stay with Rome.

Some of our Roman Catholic friends attempted to persuade us to remain with Rome by appealing to Rome's numerical superiority, "but how can one billion Roman Catholics be wrong?" One cannot of course prove truth by force of numbers, after all by the year 2,000 Moslems will outnumber Christians - what then? Besides, this line of reasoning was justly condemned by Pope Pius IX in his *Syllabus of Errors* number 60, (1864) "To one who says, 'Authority is nothing else but numbers and the sum total of material strength,' let him be anathema."

A number of times, during our two years of praying, reading and research, we attended Russian and Greek liturgies only to walk out half way, feeling completely alienated. Our emotional side desperately wanted to stay with what was familiar and comfortable, however; after a short period of time we would say, "but the Orthodox are right". Our intellect would always deny us the luxury of giving in to our emotions. When we look back it was only the grace of God that urged us on like an insistent call because, when we started to investigate the Orthodox Church, we did not have a warm circle of Orthodox friends gently prodding us in the right direction. It was a painful lonely journey but at least the pain kept our motives pure.

In a beautiful moving ceremony amidst the flickering candles, warm hues of the icons and the lingering fragrance of incense, we were received into the Orthodox Church by Chrismation on Lazarus Saturday, 1995. We were orphans no longer. The traditional church that we loved and longed for was here. The sacraments, which Rome has always recognized the validity of and which are so important in our spiritual lives, were all there and conferred in an unchanged manner. For instance, leavened bread for the Eucharist which Rome also used for the first 800 years[12] and following Christ's command: "Suffer the little children to come unto me, and forbid them not; of such is the kingdom of God." Mark 10:14, granting communion to infants which Rome practiced until the 12th century.[13] It was amazing to discover all the rich traditions and practices which Rome had gradually shed over the centuries, were still very much part of the Orthodox Church.

During those two years of prayer and study, we frequently attended the Divine Liturgy which we grew to love, gradually losing our sense of alienation. On one occasion, during a visit from the Bishop, I witnessed the Orthodox rite of confession. This took place before the

---

12 Jungman, Vol l, page 84.

13 Ibid., Vol. II, page 385.

iconostasis and at the end, the Bishop embraced the penitent and I remember being truly struck by the love and tenderness displayed. Like any church, the Orthodox Church is not without her problems. Controversies and problems have been with the church from the beginning; one only has to read the Pauline Epistles for evidence of that. However, in spite of it all, she has remained a splendid witness to Christian tradition and zealously guards all her traditions and liturgy against change, thus affording her faithful with an enormous sense of permanence and tranquility in their spiritual lives.

The Orthodox Church has retained the essential character of the catholicity of the early church echoed by St. Ignatius of Antioch, (martyred, circa. 110 A.D.) "Where the bishop is to be seen, there let all his people be; just as wherever Jesus Christ is present, we have the catholic Church". Saint Jerome describes it thus:

> It is not the case that there is one church at Rome and another in all the world beside. Gaul and Britian, Africa and Persia, India and the East worship one Christ and observe one rule of truth. If you ask for authority, the world outweighs its capital. Wherever there is a bishop, whether it be at Rome or at Engubium, whether it be Constantinople or at Rhegium, whether it be at Alexandria or at Zoan, his dignity is one and his priesthood is one. Neither the command of wealth nor the lowliness of poverty makes him more a bishop or less a bishop. All alike are successors of the apostles. (Letter CXLVI to Evangelus)

The local church with its bishop contains the totality of the universal church. This model is far removed from the Roman Catholic concept, whereby the local church is Catholic only because it is a segment of a greater corporate body and where the glory of the universal church, is spotlighted with glaring intensity on the office of one bishop, hence Pope Pius IX could exclaim, "Witness of tradition; there is only one; that's me".[14] In fact, the Church of the Seven Ecumenical Councils called for an equilibrium that we find in Canon 34 of the Apostolic Canons. These canons date from the first half of the fourth century and mirror the practices of the pre-Nicaean Church where Rome enjoyed a primacy of honour - first among equals (primus inter pares). These canons were translated into Latin by Dionysius Exiguus in the late 5th century and were widely accepted in the West. Canon 34 reads as follow:

> The bishops of every nation must acknowledge him who is first among them and account him as their head and do nothing of consequence without his consent; but each may do those things which concern his own parish and the country places which belong to it. But neither let him who is the first do anything without the consent of all. For so

[14] The Vatican Council 1869 - 1870, page 355, Dom Cuthbert Butler, Collins & Harvill Press, London. (Archbishop Felix Dupanloup of Orleans and Archbishop Georges Darboy of Paris, both recorded this famous remark in their diaries a few hours after the Pope uttered it on June 18th, 1870).

there will be oneness of mind and God will be glorified through the Lord in the Holy Spirit.[15]

In many ways western Christians live in a world where their sole points of reference are Roman Catholic or Protestant. The Protestant revolt that ignited Western Europe and the Roman Catholic counter Reformation, define the boundaries of our religious experience. When we look outside these religious boundaries, many of us are constrained by our culture. With these cultural blinkers the Orthodox Church can look very ethnic or very different - in fact many of these so-called differences were once common practices in Western Churches.

What follows is the result of two years of study. It is difficult to enter into controversial issues without arousing disagreement and resentment. There were times when I was intimidated into thinking that perhaps I should not write this book lest I would be considered anti-Catholic - which I am certainly not. As an Orthodox Christian I share with Roman Catholics the belief that the three cornerstones of the Protestant Revolt i.e. Sola Scriptura, Sola Fide and Imputed Righteousness are totally wrong, but this belief however, does not make us anti-Protestant. All Christians believe that the Jewish people were wrong in rejecting Christ as the Messiah, but this does not make us anti-Semitic.

---

15 Byzantine Theology, page 80, John Meyendorff, New York, St. Vladimir Seminary Press, 1974.

CHAPTER I

The Bishops of Rome invite close scrutiny from Orthodox Christians because they are claiming prerogatives of supreme universal jurisdiction over the Orthodox Church. Pius XI explains in his encyclical *Lux Veritatis,* when together with the Blessed Virgin Mary he pines for Orthodox Christians who have been, "unhappily led away from the unity of the Church, and therefore from her Son, whose Vicar on earth We are. May they return to the common Father,.....may they all turn to Us, who have indeed a fatherly affection for them all, and who gladly make them Our Own". When Rome makes such claims, however warmly made, she must risk suffering the proverbial lot of the claimant by occasionally having his claim rejected and more so if his claim appears especially exalted.

In this book I have relied on the best scholarship available on early church history to illustrate Rome's role in the early church, specifically in the ecumenical councils and how she was perceived by the Church at large. Also, I have relied heavily on Roman Catholic historians as they comment on the major issues such as, Papal Infallibility. It may come as a surprise to some Catholics that before the defining of the definition in 1870, many of the church's most respected historians roundly denounced it as untenable.

It should be stated that the liturgical revolution within the Catholic Church was only the catalyst, certainly not the reason for moving to the Orthodox Church. Rather it was that the claims of the Papacy did not stand close historical analysis, which ultimately called into question the doctrine of Papal Infallibility.

Especially significant and revealing for me, was Rome's role and place in the Seven Ecumenical Councils and how those councils through their documents and actions perceived Rome's position.

Even though she has veered both in her structures and traditions from the Early Church, the Roman Catholic Church's enormous contribution to Western Society must be recognized and appreciated. She founded the first universities e.g., Oxford, Cambridge, the University of Paris, countless thousands of hospitals and orphanages and inspired the building of the great gothic cathedrals. Special tribute must be paid to the thousands of missionaries who toiled in the New World to spread the Gospel; leaving place names like San Francisco, San Diego, Corpus Christi and Santa Barbara as a perpetual testament of their piety. We remain grateful to the Church of Rome for the many spiritual truths she passed on to us and maintain a close relationship with her as many members of our family and friends, both lay and clerical, are within her fold.

CHAPTER II

Peter and the Papacy

Inscribed in Latin around the base of the giant dome in the interior of St. Peter's in Rome are the words: TU ES PETRUS ET SUPER HANC PETRAM AEDIFICABO ECCLESIAM MEAM ET TIBI DABO CLAVES REGNI CAELORUM - Thou art Peter; and upon this rock I will build My church.....and I will give to thee the keys of the kingdom of heaven. In this brief passage from St. Matthew's gospel 16:18-19 lies the very basis, the seminal seed for papal supremacy and for the vast majority of Roman Catholics, the first and main line of defense in supporting the Papacy. This is the very basis of all Catholic dogma, for everything rests on this claim of Christ's commission to Peter where he is said to have been appointed ruler of His Church.

Such a momentous empowerment on the person of Peter by Christ Himself, should have resonated throughout the entire Church; the enormity of the commission sweeping away any ambiguity and reflecting complete unanimity among the Fathers of the Church as to its meaning. As Pope Leo XIII writes in his encyclical *Satis Cognitum* it is "the venerable and constant belief of every age" recognized "always and everywhere and by all". This encyclical insists that the papal claims based on the Petrine text from Matthew's gospel are *jure divino* (by Divine law), which means that the Bishops of Rome enjoyed universal jurisdiction and the charism of infallible teaching from the very beginning. *Satis Cognitum* pointedly excludes the theory that papal power was a result of gradual development, for it states that, "in the decree of the Vatican Council as to the nature and authority of the primacy of the Roman Pontiff, no newly conceived opinion is set forth, but the venerable and constant belief of every age", i.e. it was all there from the beginning, or it wasn't there at all.

The Orthodox Church had always maintained, however; that the Early Church saw no theological basis in Matthew 16:18-19 to support the claims of Rome; stating rather, that most of the Early Church saw in this passage that Christ was building His Church, not on the person of Peter, but on Peter's confession of faith and therefore, was not declaring him to be the sole foundation of His Church. A much quoted survey compiled by Roman Catholic scholar Jean de Launoy, [16]finds that there are seventeen fathers who thought of the rock as Peter; forty-four thought it referred to Peter's confession; sixteen thought Christ himself was the rock, while eight thought the rock represented all the apostles, i.e. 80% of the fathers did not recognize the person of Peter as the rock. Archbishop Kenrick; of St. Louis, used this argument in vain when he opposed the defining of Papal Infallibility at the First Vatican Council.[17] The following is a sample of what some of the Church Fathers had to say regarding Peter's confession being the rock:

> See what praises follow this faith. 'Thou art Peter, and upon this rock I will build this Church'. What

16 *Epist.* Vii., Opp. Vol. V., pt.2. p. 99 : Geneva, 1731.

17 Documenta, Vol.1, page 195 f. Friedrich.

meaneth, 'Upon this rock I will build My Church'? Upon this faith; upon this that has been said, 'Thou art the Christ, the Son of the Living God. Upon this rock' saith He 'I will build My Church'. St. Augustine, Homily X on John V. 1-3.

'And I say unto thee, Thou art Peter, and upon this rock I will build My Church', that is, on the faith of his confession. St John, Chrysostom Homily LIV on Matthew XIV.13.

Faith is the foundation of the Church, for it was not of the person but of the faith of St. Peter that it was said that the gates of hell should not prevail against it; it is the confession of faith that has vanquished hell. Jesus Christ is the Rock. He did not deny the grace of His name when He called him Peter, because he borrowed from the rock the constancy and solidity of his faith. Endeavor then, thyself to be a rock - thy rock is thy faith, and faith is the foundation of the Church. If thou art a rock, thou shalt be in the Church for the Church is built upon the rock.....St. Ambrose, On the Incarnation.

Rock is the unity of faith, not the person of Peter. St. Cyprian, De Catholicae Ecclesiae Unitate, cap. 4-5

It should be pointed out that the famous epigram, attributed to St. Augustine *"Roma locuta est; causa finita est"*, (Rome has spoken, the case is closed) is completely untrue. Augustine made no such statement. The origin of this remark is supposedly drawn from sermon 131:10 which is as follows: "Already two councils have sent to the Apostolic See concerning this matter, and rescripts have come from hence. The case is concluded; would that error soon cease...." Augustine is stating that two African Councils have rendered a judgment against the Pelagians and they were sent to Rome, "from thence rescripts have come; the cause is finished." The African church and Rome have condemned Pelagius and that is the end of the matter.

When Pope Zosimus restored Pelagius, Augustine and the African church did not hesitate to vigorously oppose him by calling a council at Carthage where Pelagius was anathematized. The council then appealed to the tribunal of the Roman Emperor Honorius who issued an imperial edict banishing the Pelagians from Rome. Pope Zosimus ultimately backed down and issued his own condemnation. Catholic scholars uncovered this error over 100 years ago and Catholic historians like Warren H. Carroll are in full concurrence.[18] The popularity of this mythical remark (*Roma Locuta est; causa finita est)* Rome has spoken, the case is closed; is that it is so neat, so concise and so conclusive. It even has a nice ring to it - like a worn cliche - that slides effortlessly into our consciousness and distorts our perception of history.

St. Augustine had ample opportunity in his actions and vast literary works to express his belief in the supreme jurisdiction of Rome. Of all the Fathers of the Church, St. Agustine wrote the most on church unity and authority. He wrote 75 chapters to the separated

---

18 The Building of Christendom, Vol. 2, pages 99 - 100, Warren H. Carroll, Christendom College Press, Front Royal, Va. 1987.

Donatists on the *Unity of the Church*, using all sorts of arguments to urge them to return to communion. Of the necessity of communion with Rome, or Rome as a centre of unity, or Rome's supreme authority, there is not one single word. It should be mentioned that when St. Augustine refers to Rome as the "Apostolic See", he is not conferring any special power or authority in the title, for "The Christian Society is diffused by the propagation all over the world by the Apostolic Sees and the succession of bishops in them."[19]

As with the Fathers of the early church, St. Augustine recognized the General Councils as the supreme authority of the church. In his dispute with the Donatists about re-baptism, he does not condemn Cyprian for refusing to submit to the Bishop of Rome, for he writes that a General Council has not issued a judgment on the subject and that St. Cyprian would, "undoubtedly have yielded if at any time the truth of the question had been placed beyond all dispute by the investigation and decree of a General Council".[20] With respect to the correct baptismal formula, Augustine says: "We ourselves would not dare to assert anything such unless we were supported by the most harmonious authority of the universal Church".[21] We can "declare with the confidence of a fearless voice that which under Government of our Lord God and Saviour Jesus Christ has been ratified by a Council of the universal

---

19 Retractationes, 1:21. P. L. 32: 618.

20 De Bapt. Contra Donatistas, lib, (Migne) ii. Patrologiae Latinae Cursus Completus, 43:129.

21 Ibid.,

Church".[22] In response to one of its deposed priests appealing to Pope Zosimus for reinstatement, the North African Church asserted its independent jurisdiction at the Synod of Carthage on the 1st of May 418, by passing the following canon:

> If priests, deacons and inferior clerics complain of a sentence of their own bishops, they shall, with the consent of their bishop, have recourse to the neighbouring bishops, who shall settle the dispute. If they desire to make a further appeal, it must only be to their primates or to African Councils. But whoever appeals to a court on the other side of the sea may not again be received into communion by anyone in Africa.[23]

To St. Augustine, appealing to a judgment from Rome to a universal Council of the Church was perfectly legitimate, as he admits in his *Epistle 43*, "Supposing those bishops who judged at Rome were not good judges, there remained still a plenary Council of the universal Church where the cause could be sifted with the judges themselves, so that if they were convicted of having judged wrongly their sentence could be annulled."[24]

---

22 De Bapt. Contra Donatistas, lib, vii. P.L. 43:242, 243.

23 Sacrorum Conciliorum Nova Et Amplissima Collectio, G.D. Mansi, iii, 726, Florence, 1759 - 63.

24 Patrologiae Latinae Cursus Completus, 33:169, J.P. Migne, ed., Paris, 1844 - 66.

PETER AND THE PAPACY

Some Church Fathers regarded the word "Rock" as referring to Christ or the faith of the Apostles, not Peter alone.

> Therefore Peter is so called from the rock; not the rock from Peter; as Christ is not called Christ from the Christian, but the Christian from Christ. "Therefore," he saith, "Thou art Peter; and upon this Rock" which thou hast confessed, upon this Rock which thou hast acknowledged, saying, "Thou art the Christ, the Son of the living God, will I build My Church:" that is upon Myself, the Son of the living God, "will I build My Church." I will build thee upon Myself, not Myself upon thee. For men who wish to be built upon men, said, "I am of Paul; and I of Apollos; and I of Cephas," (1 Cor. 1:12) who is Peter. But others who do not wish to be built upon Peter, but upon the Rock, said, "But I am of Christ." And when the Apostle Paul ascertained that he was chosen, and Christ despised, he said, "Is Christ divided? Was Paul crucified for you? Or were ye baptized in the name of Paul?" (1 Cor. 1:13) And, as not in the name of Paul, so neither in the name of Peter; but in the name of Christ: that Peter might be built upon the Rock, not the Rock upon Peter. Saint Augustine Sermon XXVI Matt. XIV, 25.

> Christ is the Rock Who granted to His apostles that they should be called rock. God has founded His Church on this Rock, and it is from this Rock that Peter has been named. St. Jerome, 6th Book on Matthew.

CHAPTER II

> I believe that by the Rock you must understand the unshaken faith of the apostles. St. Hilary, Second Book on the Trinity.

> The word "Rock" has only a denominative value - it signifies nothing but the steadfast and firm faith of the apostles. St. Cyril, Patriarch of Alexandria, Of the Trinity, 4th Book.

> Peter and John were equal in dignity and honour. Christ is the foundation of all - the unshakable Rock upon which we are all built as a spiritual edifice. St. Cyril of Alexandria, in his letter to Nestorius.

Furthermore, the power of binding and loosing is also given to the other apostles in Matthew 18:18 therefore, sharing the same power as Peter. While Peter was undeniably the first among the Twelve, he never acted or spoke alone but always in union with them. Thus the Early Church's understanding of Matthew 16:18-19 and the Petrine Primacy was that all bishops shared in the Petrine power. The idea that the Church is built solely on the person of Peter and that he enjoyed a supremacy over the Apostles and hence the Church is explicitly denied:

> He had not the primacy over the disciples (in discipulos) but among the disciples (in discipulis). His primacy among the disciples was the same as that of Stephen among the deacons. St. Augustine, Sermon 10 on Peter and Paul.

> As soon as Peter heard these words, 'Whom say ye that I am?' remembering his place he exercised this

primacy, a primacy of confession, not of honour; a primacy of faith, not of rank. St. Ambrose, De In Som Sacr. 4:32.

But observe how Peter does everything with the common consent; nothing imperiously. St. John Chrysostom, Homily III on Acts 1:12.

To all the apostles after His resurrection He gives equal power (parem potestatem) and says, 'As the Father sent Me so I send you'. St. Cyprian, De Unitate. 4

For neither did Peter, whom first the Lord chose... when Paul disputed with him afterwards about the circumcision, claim anything to himself insolently, nor arrogantly assume anything, so as to say that he held a primacy, and that he ought to be obeyed by novices and those lately come. St. Cyprian, Epistle LXX concerning the baptism of Heretics.

St. Cyprian also says: In the administration of the Church each bishop has the free discretion of his own will, having to account only to the Lord for his actions. None of us may set himself up as bishop of bishops, nor compel his brothers to obey him; every bishop of the Church has full liberty and complete power; as he cannot be judged by another, neither can he judge another. (in his opening address to the Council of Carthage).

Here Cyprian reminds us that the collegial structure of the Church, (all bishops sharing power) is based on Divine Law, with a pointed reproof to those bishops who would set themselves over their peers:

CHAPTER II

> .....through the changes of times and successions, the ordering of bishops and the plan of the Church flow onwards; so that the Church is founded upon the bishops, and every act of the Church is controlled by these same rulers. Since this, then, is founded on the divine law, I marvel that some, with daring temerity, have chosen to write to me as if they wrote in the name of the Church;..... Cyprian to the Lapsed. Epistle XXVI, (2).

If the Bishop of Rome was everywhere regarded as the supreme head of the church, where were the cries of heresy to such statements as those of St. Cyprian?

It has been claimed that Rome enjoyed her pre-eminence among the Patriarchal Sees because of her senior apostolic foundation, i.e. St. Peter had been martyred there. This system of apostolic ranking however, is not reflected in the positioning of the Patriarchal Sees. As the British Byzantine historian Sir Steven Runciman observes; Alexandria was senior to Antioch in spite of the fact that the Antiochene Church had St. Peter as its founder and the Alexandrian Church was founded by St. Mark. "It could not therefore be said that precedence depended upon the apostolic foundation". Furthermore, Jerusalem "the Mother of all Churches"[25] was not constituted a Patriarchal See until the Council of Chalcedon in 451. Rome's senior ranking was due primarily to political considerations as we shall see reflected in the canons of the Ecumenical Councils. "Alexandria came next because she was the second city in the Empire, the equal in size and wealth

---

[25] Mansi, iii, 588.

to Rome itself." The fact that SS. Peter and Paul were martyred there, gave Rome a "special prestige" and a "purely honourary primacy",[26] certainly not a universal jurisdiction.

Many Roman Catholic apologists ignore the writings of the Early Church Fathers, who were equally well versed in scripture and focus solely on their interpretation of Matthew 16:18-19. "And I say unto thee: That thou art Peter and upon this rock I will build my church..... And I will give thee the keys of the kingdom of heaven....". To them it is so clear, what else could it mean? They will even delve into the Old Testament to find supporting evidence for the imagery of the "keys". In doing so they lapse into the practice of "Sola Scriptura" (by scripture alone), that they accuse Protestants of committing - by ignoring the mind of the Early Church in favour of their own subjective judgment. In addition, they anticipate their own conclusion in their initial premise when they associate any reference by Early Church Fathers, of Peter as head of the apostles, the seat of Peter, Peter and the keys etc., as pointing to evidence of Rome's supreme universal authority.

---

[26] The Eastern Schism; a Study of the Papacy and the Eastern Churches During the XI and XII Centuries - page 12 and 13, Sir Steven Runciman, Oxford, 1955.

CHAPTER II

THE COUNCIL OF JERUSALEM - THE BIRTH OF CONCILIAR TRADITION

At the Council of Jerusalem as recorded in Acts 15, we see the beginnings of the conciliar nature of the Church. Upon their return to Antioch from their missionary journey, Paul and Barnabas brought up the persistent problem of Gentile converts and circumcision. A serious controversy erupted between Paul and Barnabas and "certain men from Judaea". The question of whether Gentile Christians should submit to the rite of circumcision only led to a deeper question as to how much, if any, of the Mosaic Law Christians should be compelled to accept. A council was called in Jerusalem to hear Paul and Barnabas and to issue a declaration. As Bishop of Jerusalem it was James who presided and who rendered the Councils final judgment - not Peter. After hearing Peter, James addressed the Council:

> Simon hath related how God first visited to take of the Gentiles a people to his name.....For which cause I judge that they, who from among the Gentiles are converted to God, are not to be disquieted. But that we write unto them.....(Acts 15:14-20).

As a result of this Council a declaration was issued by the "Apostles, elders and the brethren", that absolved Gentile Christians from undergoing the rite of circumcision as a condition of entering the Church. However, more important was the decision that the imposition of the Mosaic Law as a whole was not to be made as a requirement for Gentile converts to Christianity. These declarations saved the Church from embarking on the false Pharasaical road of salvation by works.

Understandably the Roman Catholic Church has always taught that Peter presided at the Council but, James held the Episcopal See of Jerusalem and as we see in Acts 15, as befitting his role he (James) summed up the discussion and rendered the judgment. Hence, the obvious conclusion is that St. Peter's fellow Apostles and leaders of the Jerusalem Christian community, did not view him as the sole foundation stone of the Church. James' pivotal role at this Council was recognized by early Church Fathers such as John Chrysostom:

> 'Then all the multitude kept silence,' etc.(v.12.) There was no arrogance in the Church. After Peter, Paul speaks, and none silences him: James waits patiently, not starts up (for the next word). Great orderliness (of the proceedings). No word speaks John here, no word the other apostles, but held their peace, for James was invested with the chief rule, and I think it no hardship. So clean was their soul from love of glory. 'And after that they had held their peace, James answered,' etc. (v.13.) Peter indeed spoke more strongly, but James here more mildly: for thus it behooves one in high authority, to leave what is unpleasant for others to say, while he himself appears in the milder part. (Upon the Acts of the Apostles, 33d Homily).

CHAPTER II

The famous early church historian Eusebius wrote: "This James, whom the early Christians named the Righteous because of his outstanding virtue, was the first as the records tell us, to be elected to the Episcopal throne of the Jerusalem church. Clement, in *Outlines Book 6*, puts it thus: "Peter, James, and John, after the Ascension of the Savior, did not claim preeminence because the Savior had specially honoured them but chose James the Righteous as Bishop of Jerusalem." Eusebius, *(The History of the Church)*.[27]

Contemporary scholarship confirms that the use of Matthew 16:18-19 as a theological basis for Roman Primacy is not found in the records of the Infant Church. In the book *The Early Church*, which has become almost a standard text on the subject, Henry Chadwick, Regius Professor of Divinity at Oxford and Cambridge Universities states that:

> But before the third century there was no call for a sustained, theoretical justification of this leadership. All were brethren, but the church in Rome was accepted as first among equals. The 'Petrine text' of Matthew 16:18, 'Thou art Peter and upon this rock I will build my Church', cannot be seen to have played any part in the story of Roman leadership and authority before the middle of the third century when the passionate disagreement between Cyprian of Carthage and Stephen of Rome about baptism apparently led Stephen to invoke the text as part of his defense against Cyprian. But it was not until Damasus in 382 that this Petrine text

27 The History of the Church - 11.1, Eusebius.

> seriously began to become important as providing a theological and scriptural foundation on which claims to Primacy were based. .....From Damasus onwards there is a marked crescendo in the expression of the claims made by the bishops of Rome.[28]

Collin Morris Professor of Medieval History of Southampton University England puts it this way:

> The title deeds of the Roman Church were the familiar Petrine texts, but these were not interpreted as applying solely to the Pope. Thus the declaration of Matthew 16:18, 'on this rock I will build my church', was usually regarded as a reference not to Peter, but to Christ or the confession of faith, and it was held that the powers of binding and loosing belonged to the apostles (Matt. 18:18) while being given principally to Peter, as Matthew 16:19 implies.[29]

Many historians have remarked that it was Paul rather than Peter who established Rome as a major Christian city and therefore should be regarded as its founder.[30] For many centuries Rome was always known as the city of SS. Peter and Paul, recognizing an equal

---

28 The Early Church - page 237, Henry Chadwick, Penguin Books, Revised Edition, 1993.

29 The Papal Monarchy, Oxford History of the Church, page 208, Clarendon Press, Oxford, 1991.

30 Jerusalem and Rome - pages 23 - 36, Henry Chadwick, Hans von Campenhausen, Philadelphia, 1966.

debt to both, however, as the papal claims to Petrine power became more insistent, Paul's name as a co-founder faded.

ROME'S CLAIMS TO UNIVERSAL JURISDICTION IN THE EARLY CHURCH

The usual evidence produced to prove Rome's supremacy in the immediate post New Testament Church is the letter of Clement, Bishop of Rome to the Corinthians. The purpose of this letter, written in the last decade of the first century, was to address the trouble in the Church of Corinth where they had deposed their leaders and had installed others in their place. The letter, rather than being issued from Clement personally, is presented corporately, "From the colony of the Church of God at Rome, To the colony of the Church of God at Corinth". The letter is written with a fraternal exhortation and does not appeal to any Petrine texts or claim any extraordinary jurisdiction. Had it done so, the letter would have been written in a very different style.

Another evidence which Rome uses to support her claims of universal jurisdiction in the early church is a passage from the work *Adversus Haereses* - Against Heresies by St. Irenaeus, Bishop of Lyons (Circa. A.D. 140-202). All we have of this Greek work is a Latin translation. The translation of this passage (Adv. Haer. III, 3, 2.) has been hotly debated over the centuries. This Latin passage reads as follows:

Ad hane ecclesiam propter potentiorem principalitatem necesse est omnem convenire ecclesiam, hoc est, eos qui sunt undique fideles, in qua semper ab his qui sunt undique, conservata est ea quae est ab apotolis traditio.

A typical Roman Catholic translation of this famous passage is as follows:

For with this Church, because of its superior origin, all Churches must agree, that is, all the faithful in the whole world; and it is in her that the faithful everywhere have maintained the Apostolic tradition.[31]

Other translations read:

For it is necessary that every church come together with this church on account of its greater antiquity.

Much of the controversy centres on the Latin word *convenire*,- the root of our word "convene" - which the Roman Catholic source translates as "must agree", supporting its claim of supreme jurisdiction. The other translation puts it as "come together", while some sources translate it as "all churches must turn to", "all churches must have recourse to", or "must be in harmony with". It should be pointed out that the word "agree" in the hierarchy of possible meanings of the word *convenire* in the Latin dictionary - mine is

---

31 The Faith of the Early Fathers, Vol. L, page 90 (210). W.A. Jurgens, The Liturgical Press, Collegeville, Minnesota,

Cassell's - the translations "to come together", "collect", "who belong", "to visit", "to meet", are more immediate. The translation "to agree with" is more metaphorical and is listed with "be congenial", "to harmonize", "be fitting". The use of the imperative word "must" in "must agree", in the Roman Catholic translation gives an imperative mood that is not there.

The exact meaning of this passage will continue to be debated until, if ever, the original Greek text surfaces. As Nicholas Afanassieff states in *The Primacy of Peter,*[32] "The sense of the remark would be", 'every local church should have recourse to the Church of Rome'. F.W. Puller in his book *Primitive Saints and the See of Rome,* states that the words *convenire ad* occurs in 26 passages in the Jerome Vulgate Bible, and the meaning in every case is "to come together" or "resort to." "It would perhaps be rash to lay down a universal negative, and to say that *convenire ad* never means 'agree with'; but as far as I am aware no such passage has ever yet been produced."[33] Irenaeus himself confirms this sense of '*convernire*' (Adv. Haer. III, 4,1.) in explaining what he had said about the Church of Rome and other churches apostolically founded:

> If at any time some simple question of detail should happen to provoke a dispute, surely the oldest churches, and those in which the Apostles lived, are the ones we should have recourse to (recurrere), and

---

32 The Primacy of Peter - page 132, John Meyendorff, Editor, St. Vladimir's Seminary Press, Crestwood, New York, 1992.

33 Primitive Saints and the See of Rome, page 26, F.W. Puller.

> they will give us something very certain, and very clear, on this case in question.

This fits the picture of the pre-Nicene Church of Rome enjoying a Primacy of Honour due to its Pauline and Petrine tradition with a jurisdiction limited to its own surrounding area as evidenced by the letter written by Ignatius of Antioch on his journey to martyrdom in Rome (circa A.D. 98-117). In his letter to the Roman Christians he writes: "to the Church that is in charge of affairs in Roman quarters". Over two hundred years later, we still see Rome as a church enjoying a primacy of honour with a limited geographical jurisdiction as evidenced in Canon 6 of the First Council of Nicea:

> Let the ancient customs in Egypt, Libya and Pentapolis prevail, that the Bishop of Alexandria have jurisdiction in all these, since the like is customary for the Bishop of Rome also. Likewise, in Antioch and the other provinces, let the Churches retain their privileges.

Ruffinus, a 4th century writer who wrote the *Ecclesiastical History*, using the term "Suburbicarian" for what was "customary for Rome", recognized Corsica, Sardinia and Southern Italy.

We now come to the famous Easter controversy in which Roman Catholics pupport to show Pope St. Victor (A.D. 189-199) exercising his supreme universal authority for the first time. The Church in Asia Minor celebrated Easter at the same time as the Jewish

Passover, i.e. on the 14th day of the Jewish month Nisan. This practice they claim was given to them by the Apostles and was therefore of ancient origin. Other Churches, Rome included, celebrated Easter on the Sunday following the full moon after the Spring Equinox. These Churches sought uniformity, therefore the early church historian Eusebius (A.D. c. 260-340), tells us that "synods and conferences of bishops were convened", in an effort to achieve uniformity. This was initiated by Pope St. Victor, who sent letters to the various Metropolitans, requesting them to convene synods in order to discuss the question. That these synods were convened by request and not by command, is evidenced by Polycrates, Bishop of Ephesus, in his letter to 'Victor and the Church of the Romans'.[34] These "synods and conferences", issued a "decree of the church in the form of letters addressed to Christians everywhere, that never on any day other than the Lord's Day should the mystery of the Lord's Resurrection of the Dead be celebrated and on that day alone we should observe the end of the Pascal fast". Eusebius goes on to tell us:

> There is extant to this day a letter from those who attended a conference in Palestine presided over by Bishop Theophilus of Caeasarea and Narcissus of Jerusalem; and from those at Rome a similar one, arising out of the same controversy, which names Victor as bishop. There are others from the Pontic bishops presided over by Palmas as the senior from the Gallic province over which Irenaeus presided,

---

[34] Eusibius, V. 24.

> and from the bishops in Osrhoene and the cities of that region. There are also personal letters from Bishop Bacchyllus of Corinth and very many more, who voiced one and the same opinion and judgment and gave the same vote. All these laid down one single rule - the rule already stated.[35]

Therefore, the decree came from these councils not from Pope St. Victor. Furthermore, we see Pope St. Victor's name listed matter-of-factly along with all the others - he doesn't even get first mention but is listed after the bishop of Palestine. Most unlikely if he commanded the convening of the council.

The Asian bishops headed by Polycrates, Bishop of Ephesus, refused to heed the decree and a dispute broke out between him and Pope St. Victor who demanded submission. The Churches of Asia also had Apostolic origins as Polycrates reminded Pope St. Victor in a measured, dignified response:

> We for our part keep the day scrupulously, without addition or subtraction. For in Asia great luminaries sleep who shall rise again....Philip.....John who leant back on the Lord's breast.....Polycarp. All these kept the 14th day of the month as the beginning of the Paschal festival in accordance with the Gospel.....and going carefully through all Holy Scripture, am not scared of threats. Better people than I have said, 'We must obey God rather than men'.

---

35 Ibid.,, V.23.

CHAPTER II

Eusebius writes, "Thereupon Victor, head of the Roman Church, attempted at one stroke to cut off from the common unity all the Asian dioceses, together with the neighboring churches, on the ground of hetrodoxy.....". The key word here of course, is the word attempted. If we decide to do something and it is within our power to do it, it is done. If however, it is not in our immediate power and we still wish to do it, then we make an attempt. This is what Pope St. Victor did when he attempted to excommunicate his fellow bishops and as with all attempts, we sometimes succeed and sometimes fail - Pope St. Victor failed. As Eusebius tells us:

> But this was not to the taste of all the bishops: they replied with a request that he would turn his mind to the things that make for peace and unity and love towards his neighbours. We still possess the words of these men, who very sternly rebuked Victor. Among them was Irenaeus, who wrote on behalf of the Christians for whom he was responsible in Gaul.[36]

The crisis abated with the Asian Churches keeping their Easter calendar. It is interesting to note that Irenaeus relates that St. Polycarp of Smyrna had visited Rome some 40 years earlier. At that time, Pope Anicetas had tried to persuade the great bishop to adopt Rome's Easter calendar to no avail. "Though the position was such, they remained in communion with each other". Note that Irenaeus does not say that

---

36 Ibid., V.24.

Polycarp remained in communion with Rome but rather that they "remained in communion with each other". Ultimately, the uniformity in the Easter observance that Rome and her sister churches sought, was gradually enforced by the general councils of the Church.

Most Roman Catholics, when they think of the Early Church think of Rome, the Popes, the Martyrs, the Catacombs and the Colosseum. This view is perfectly understandable, because for Roman Catholics or Protestants their spiritual genesis lies in Rome, i.e. Rome was the centre of Western Christianity. The Early Church however, was overwhelmingly Eastern and Greek. They had the greatest population density and its people were better educated and more sophisticated than their western brethren. The East could claim forty-four churches of apostolic origin, verses one for the West. The West was not the centre of Christianity, but for many hundreds of years was a missionary field and with the barbarian incursions had become a cultural backwater. The East held four of the five patriarchates, i.e. Constantinople, Alexandria, Antioch and Jerusalem; two of these, Alexandria and Antioch, contained the first schools of biblical interpretation. The Seven Great Ecumenical Councils were all held in the East, with an overwhelming presence of eastern bishops as we shall see in the next chapter.

CHAPTER III

The Seven Ecumenical Councils

Summoned by the Roman Emperor Constantine in the year 325, the Bishops converged on the town of Nicea - modern day Iznik - just outside Constantinople, for the first great Ecumenical Council with many of them bearing the wounds of persecution. Men such as St. Paphnutius and Potoman Bishops of Egypt, both of whom were blinded in one eye and crippled from torture and Paul of Neo-Caesarea, unable to use his burned hands. Also, great luminaries of the Church, such as St. Nicholas Bishop of Smyrna and St. Athanasius the Great, made their way to the council. Of the 270 - 300 bishops in attendance only five were from the west - Caecilian of Carthage, Domnus of Pannonia (Austria), Nicasius of Gaul (France), Mark of Calabria (Italy) and Ossius of Cordoba (Spain) who was an imperial councilor. Sylvester, Bishop of Rome, excused himself on account of his old age and sent two priests Vito and Vincent as observers. Some Roman Catholic books such as *The Story of the Church,*[37] claim that the Emperor Constantine only summoned the council with the consent of Pope Sylvester. As Catholic Historian Leo Donald Davis S.J. points out in his book, *The Seven*

---

37 The Story of the Church - page 87, Reverend George Johnson, Reverend Jerome D Hannan, Sister M Dominica, Tan Books, Rockford, Illinois, 1980.

Ecumenical Councils, this was a legend which surfaced in the seventh and eight centuries and that it was Constantine alone who summoned the council.[38]

This first great council of the Church, called to deal with the Arian heresy, became a blueprint for the remaining six ecumenical councils, i.e. they were all called by the Roman Emperor, were all held in the east, all the proceedings were conducted in Greek, were overwhelmingly attended by eastern bishops and with papal legates representing the Pope. The Pope never attended an ecumenical council. In fact, the Second Ecumenical Council, (First Constantinople) was called without the knowledge of the Pope and in the case of the Fourth and Fifth Ecumenical Councils (Chalcedon and Constantinople II against their express wishes.

Thus we will see that the early church was conciliar in its government, that the ecumenical councils represented the highest judicial body of the church, that these councils were not called to advise the Bishop of Rome and that the Bishop of Rome did not enjoy veto power. Nowhere in the canons or creeds of these councils do we find any recognition of Rome's claim to supreme universal jurisdiction. None of the Church Fathers or General Councils settled doctrinal disputes by appealing to an infallible pope. Claims of infallibility by a single bishop would have been incomprehensible. Furthermore, the idea that the Bishop of Rome was superior to a council of the church and that a council was only ecumenical because the Bishop of Rome alone

---

38 The Seven Ecumenical Councils (325 - 787) - page 56, Leo Donald Davis S.J, The Liturgical Press, Collegeville, Minnesota.

confirmed its decrees was unknown. In fact all five Patriarchs, Rome, Constantinople, Alexandria, Antioch and Jerusalem had to confirm the decrees.

THE SECOND ECUMENICAL COUNCIL

In 381 A.D. the Emperor Theodosius I, summoned a council of eastern bishops without the knowledge of the pope. This became known as the First Council of Constantinople (The Second Ecumenical Council) and the first president of this council was St. Meletius Bishop of Antioch, who was not in communion with Rome. This council ended the long Trinitarian debate by declaring the equality of the Holy Spirit with the Father and the Son. It also made alterations to the Creed of Nicea which became the Nicean-Constantinopilitan Creed. The third canon of the council gave the Bishop of Constantinople precedence of honour over all bishops except the Bishop of Rome, "because Constantinople is the New Rome". Of this canon, Leo Donald Davis S.J in his book *The First Seven Ecumenical Councils (325-787)*, says that, "Though the canon was not directed against Rome, no notice was taken of the claim of its bishop to a primacy among bishops based on his succession from Peter, head of the Apostles."[39]

While the British historian, Henry Chadwick, notes that, "although it conceded that Rome was the first See of Christendom, it implied that Roman primacy

[39] Ibid., page 128.

depended on the city's secular standing".[40] The council also proclaimed a creed that was essentially the creed of Nicea. At its conclusion the council fathers requested the Emperor to seal their decisions and Theodosius gave them legal effect. While the Eastern Church recognized this council to be ecumenical, Rome only belatedly did so in the 6th century.

It has been argued that the bishop of Rome was not invited or even notified because the Council was not intended to be ecumenical. This line of reasoning is specious however, when we reflect that a good number of councils were only declared ecumenical by succeeding ones – as this one was at the Council of Chalcedon (451). Furthermore, without Rome's notification or presence, it felt itself free to declare dogma, make alterations to the Creed of Nicea and change the Patriarchal ranking.

THE THIRD ECUMENICAL COUNCIL

On the 25th of December 1931, Pope Pius XI issued an encyclical entitled, *Lux Veritatis*, (The Light of Truth) commemorating the Council of Ephesus For Pius XI this famous council proves, ".....so expressly and significantly that already, throughout the universal Church, there was a strong and common faith in the authority of the Roman Pontiff over the whole flock of Christ, an authority subject to no one and incapable of

---

[40] The Early Church - page 151, Henry Chadwick, Penguin Books, Revised Edition, 1993.

error....." A dissenting view is dismissed as, ".....a fabric of falsehood clothed with a specious appearance of truth." We will examine the Council of Ephesus with the views of *Lux Veritatis* in mind.

In 431 A.D. the Emperor Theodosius II, summoned a general council to meet at Ephesus, (The Third Ecumenical Council) to answer the heresy of Nestorius, Bishop of Constantinople, who denied that God and man had been united in one Person in Christ. As a result, he also denied that the Virgin Mary was Theotokos - Mother of God. In August 430, Pope Celestine held a synod in Rome in which he condemned Nestorius. Celestine then wrote to Cyril, Patriarch of Alexandria, informing him of the results of the council and authorizing Cyril "the authority of our See, having been combined with yours, and acting authoritatively in our stead will carry out this sentence with due severity....."[41] Upon receipt of this letter, Cyril called a council at Alexandria, in which he issued a synodal letter in the name of both Rome and Alexandria to Nestorius and attached Twelve Anathemas of his own without Rome's knowledge or sanction. If Cyril recognizes Rome's supreme authority, why does he call a council and issue a synodal letter in the name of both churches? Surely, if "there was a strong and common faith in the authority of the Roman Pontiff over the whole flock of Christ, an authority subject to no one and incapable of error....." then Rome's weight certainly would have been enough.

41 Sacrorum Conciliorum Nova Et Amplissima Collectio, 1017 - 1022, G.D. Mansi, Florence, 1759 - 1763.

CHAPTER III

Pius XI in *Lux Veritatis* asserts that: "Nor was Nestorius ignorant of the supreme authority of the Roman Bishop over the universal Church….." In point of fact, Nestorius' correspondence to Celestine proves the complete opposite; for his correspondence permeates with a sense of equality that his own See of Constantinople enjoys with that of Rome. He looks upon Celestine as a "brother" and addresses him as such: "We ought to have fraternal communications with each other in turns in order that by obtaining concord we may oppose the Devil, the enemy of peace."[42] He continues: "Let us narrate our affairs to each other as brothers to brothers."[43] In a letter to Cyril he expresses a dim view of Celestine as a theologian: "a man too simple to be able to understand acutely the sense of the dogmas."[44] *Lux Veritatis* makes the point that: "he (Cyril) addressed most dutiful letters to 'the most blessed Father Celestine, beloved of God…..' This is very misleading, for what we would consider today gushing, exaggerated forms of address was common in the correspondence of the early church as the following examples prove, e.g. Cyril addresses Nestorius' successor in Constantinople as, "My most holy and worshipful Lord, Archbishop Father Maximian."[45] Celestine's successor Sixtus III, writes to Cyril, that the whole church is indebted to him to the point that, "all

---

42 Ibid., IV, 1021.
43 Ibid., IV, 1023.
44 Ibid., V, 762.
45 Patrologiae Graecae Cursus Completus, 77:253. J.P. Migne, Ed., Paris 1844 - 1866.

are subject to you."[46] A final example of this style would be Pope St. Leo the Great's letter to the Roman Emperor, Leo Augustus, where he informs the "most glorious Emperor, from that solid Rock, on which the city of God is built", that by the power of the Holy Spirit he is preserved from all doctrinal error:

> For in your Majesties communications it is beyond doubt revealed what the Holy Spirit is working through you for the good of the whole Church, ...And hence, since I know you, venerable Prince, imbued as you are with the purest light of truth, waver in no part of the Faith, but with just and perfect judgment distinguish right from wrong and separate what is to be embraced from what is to be rejected, I beseech you not to think that my humility is to be blamed for want of competence, since my cautiousness is not only in the interest of the universal Church but also for the furtherance of your own glory,.....I am very confident of the piety of your heart in all things, and perceive that through the Spirit of God dwelling in you, you are sufficiently instructed, nor can any error delude your faith.....

To paint a picture of Cyril Bishop of Alexandria, as recognizing the supreme authority of Rome is deplorable because such a claim cannot be found in any of his writings. In fact he rejects the very theological basis for Rome's Petrine claims when he writes, "Peter

46 Mansi, V, 374.

and John were both apostles and saints and adorned with equal honours and powers." [47] In commenting on Matthew 16:18, he teaches that the word "Rock has only a denominative value - it signifies nothing but the steadfast and firm faith of the apostles" (Of the Trinity, 4th Book). Had such claims existed, it would not have been necessary to forge them. The following forgeries attributed to Cyril of Alexandria, were accepted by St. Thomas Aquinas as explained by Roman Catholic scholar Jean de Launoy: in his letter to Antonine Faure (Op., tom. V. bk. i. p. 1) says: "I deferred until the third year about certain testimonies attributed to Cyril of Alexandria which St. Thomas received in authority. .....These testimonies are thus read in St. Thomas, and first, indeed, in *fourth Sent.* dist. xxiv. quaes. iii. art. ii.: 'Besides,', he, St. Cyril, Bishop of Alexandria, says, "that we may remain members of our head, the Apostolic See of the Roman Pontiffs, it is our duty to seek what we ought to believe and hold, venerating him and asking him for all things, since it is his duty alone to blame, to correct, to determine, to dispose, to loosen, and bind, in place of Him Who created him, and gave His own fullness to no other than to him alone, to whom by the divine law of all bow the head, even the leaders of the world, as if they obey the Lord Jesus Christ Himself." Scholars today recognize that these statements attributed to Cyril are totally spurious.

A well known three volume work of Catholic apologetics *Radio Replies*, makes the claim that the

---

[47] P.G. Migne, 76:65.

Council of Ephesus declared their acceptance of the popes supremacy over the church:

> The Council of Epheseus in 431, embracing all Bishops and not even held at Rome, decreed "No one can doubt, indeed it is known to all ages, that Peter, Prince and Head of the Apostles and Foundation of the Catholic Church, received the keys of the kingdom from Christ our Redeemer, and that to this day and always he lives in his successors exercising judgment".[48]

This is very misleading as one is given the impression that the Council of Ephesus itself produced this statement in its formal deliberations. Actually, the above statement was made by a papal legate, a priest named Philip, at the third session of Cyril's (Patriarch of Alexandria) council forming part of the legates subscription to the deposition of Nestorius. Thus a lone papal legate made the declaration, not the council itself. None of the Seven Ecumenical Councils ever issued such a statement. In *Lux Veritatis*, Pius XI, while admitting that the statement belongs to the legate Philip attempts to draw some benefit from it because no objections were raised. Leo Donald Davis S.J comments however, "The bishops accepted the legates subscription to the acts as expressing the adherence of

---

48 Radio Replies - Volume 1, page 79, Fathers Rumble and Carty, Tan Books, Rockford, Illinois, 1979.

the West to the Councils decisions and began to refer to their assembly as ecumenical."[49]

Three months before the Council of Ephesus had been convened, Pope Celestine had excommunicated Nestorius for heresy. The Council however, completely ignored the Pope's excommunication and treated Nestorius as Patriarch of Constantinople in good standing. The Council then proceeded to examine the evidence and pronounced its own sentence: "The holy Synod ..... to Nestorius the new Judas: Know that for thy impius doctrines thou wast deposed by the holy Synod agreeably to the laws of the Church ......"[50] Ignoring the excommunication pronounced by Pope Celestine, Nestorius was addressed as the, "most religious Bishop of Constantinople during his trial." After being judged and sentenced by the Council of Ephesus, he was the "new Judas" and was anathematized and excommunicated. In his encyclical *Lux Veritatis,* Pope Pius XI defends the idea that Rome's judgment of Nestorius was not judged afresh by the Council, but that the Council Fathers merely ratified the sentence already passed by Pope Celestine:

> But some writers of the past age and of more recent days, seeking to evade the luminous authority of the documents which we have cited, have given the following account of the whole matter, which they often set forth.....the council afterwards summoned at Ephesus took the matter already judged and

---

49 Leo Donald Davis, page 157.

50 Mansi, IV, 1227.

> together condemned by the Apostolic See, and judged it afresh from the beginning and decreed it by its supreme authority what must be believed about it by all. From this they say it may be gathered that an Ecumenical Council is possessed of rights altogether more powerful and more valid than the authority of the Roman Bishop. But in this they have constructed a fabric of falsehood clothed with a specious appearance of truth.....it must be observed that when the Emperor Theodosius, acting also in the name of his colleague Valentinian, summoned the Ecumenical Council, the judgment of Celestine had not yet arrived at Constantinople, and nothing was known about it there.....(Celestine) delegated and proclaimed his legates who were to preside at the Council, namely, the Patriarch Cyril, the Bishops Archadius and Projectus, and the Priest Philip. But by acting thus the Pontiff did not leave an unjudged case to the decision of the Council.....he ordered the Fathers of the Council to execute the sentence passed by himself....."

Pope Pius XI's assertion that the judgment of Celestine, "had not arrived at Constantinople and nothing was known about it there", is just not so. It was written to Nestorius on August 11, 430[51] and the inference of course, is that had the Emperor known of Celestine's judgment he would not have called a general council; thus recognizing Rome's supreme authority. But the Emperor Theodosius, like his predecessors and his successors, recognized general councils as the supreme ruling body of the church - not the Bishop of Rome.

---

51 Ibid., IV, 1025 - 1036.

CHAPTER III

Theodosius was well aware of Celestine's judgment of Nestorius and this for him was not definitive. According to British Byzantine historian Steven Runciman, two months is more than enough time to cover the distance from Rome to Constantinople, which means Celestine's judgment would have arrived in early October. The Emperor Theodosius, issued his summons to the Council on the 19th of November. Jesuit historian Leo Donald Davis S.J agrees that of course the Emperor knew of Rome's judgment: ....."In November the Emperor, not regarding the papal condemnation as definitive, had already convoked a general council....."[52] In his letter to Cyril the Emperor clearly demonstrates that in the judgment of Nestorius, it is a general council of the Church that has supreme authority: "It is our will that the holy doctrine be discussed and examined in a sacred Synod, and that be ratified which appeareth agreeable to the right faith, whether the wrong party be pardoned by the Fathers or no.....those who everywhere preside over the Priesthood, and through whom we ourselves are and shall be professing the truth, must be judges of this matter."[53]

The famous French historian and Roman Catholic Bishop Bossuet observes, "It was fixed that all was in suspense once the authority of the universal Synod was invoked even though the sentence of the Roman Pontiff about doctrine and about persons accused of heresy had

---

52 Leo Donald Davis, page 153.

53 Mansi, IV. 1111 - 1116.

been uttered and promulgated." [54] Roman Catholic historian Bishop Maret states: "The Pope had pronounced in the affair of Nestorius a canonical judgment clothed with all the authority of his see. He had prescribed its execution. Yet, however, three months after this sentence and before its execution, all the episcopate is invited to examine afresh and to decide freely the question in dispute;….."[55]

St. Vincent of Lerins recounting of the Council of Ephesus and its condemnation of Nestorius for heresy, is a forceful statement for the General Council as the supreme governing body of the Church. As we have seen, three months prior to the convening of the Council, Pope Celestine excommunicated Nestorius however, St. Vincent makes no mention of this. For him it is the General Councils condemnation that is decisive under the leadership of St. Cyril Patriarch of Alexandria. St. Vincent lists the names of ten men whose witnesses or judgments were decisive in Nestorius' condemnation – Pope Celestine's name is not included. Due to the preponderance of Eastern bishops the testimonies of two Bishops of Rome, Felix and Julius were included to preserve the universality of the Church "…..lest Greece or the East should seem to stand alone, to prove that the Western and Latin world also have always held the same belief…." The witnesses and judgments of the ten men and the authority of the General Council is then summed up as

---

[54] Defensis Declarationis Cleri Gallicani, Gallia Orthodoxa Lib., vij., cap., ix, Bishop Bossuet. Abridged. Translation by Allies.

[55] Du Concile General, vol. i, page 183. Bishop Maret.

follows: "And that blessed council holding their doctrine, following their counsel, believing their witness, submitting to their judgment without haste without forgone conclusion, without partiality, gave their determination concerning the Rules of Faith."[56]

The evidence does not support Pius XI's declaration that Cyril Patriarch of Alexandria was a papal legate. For Pope Celestine never refers to Cyril as his legate to the Council and the Council in its correspondence to Celestine describes only Arcadius, Projectus and Philip as those who, "filled the place of the Apostolic See."[57] Monsignor Duchesne observes that Cyril's position of acting in Celestine's place, "seems clearly to have expired. Besides, the best proof that the Pope had no idea of causing himself to be represented by him is the fact that he was sending legates."[58] Dom. Chapman agrees that Cyril, "as the first bishop in the world after the Bishop of Rome, assumed the presidency of the council...... It does not appear that Celestine had commissioned Cyril to be his representative at Ephesus."[59]

The claim in *Lux Veritatis* that Celestine, "ordered the Fathers of the Council to execute the sentence passed by himself", is also not true. He certainly ordered the legates, "to execute the sentence passed by

---

56 Commonitorium of St. Vincent of Lerins, Book 1, Chapter XXX.

57 Mansi, VI, 1337.

58 The Early History of the Church, vol. III, page 243, Monsignor Louis Duchesne, John Murray, Albemarle Street W. London, 1960.

59 Bishop Gore and the Catholic Claims, page 89, Dom. John Chapman.

himself" - that was part of their function at the Council. But he was far from ordering the Fathers of the Council. His correspondence to them bears a polite diplomatic expectation that the Fathers of the Council will agree with his judgment: "We do not doubt that your Holinesses will manifest your consent to this when you perceive that what has been done was declared for the security of the universal Church."[60]

Pope Pius XI ends his Encyclical *Lux Veritatis* with a plea to the Orthodox Churches;

> We especially desire that all should implore, under the auspices of the heavenly Queen. That is to say, that she who is loved and worshipped with such ardent piety by the separated peoples of the East should not suffer them to wonder and be unhappily led away from the unity of the Church, and therefore from her Son, whose Vicar on earth We are. May they return to the common Father, whose judgment all the Fathers of the Synod of Ephesus most dutifully received, and whom they all saluted, with concordant acclamations, as "the guardian of the faith"; may they all turn to Us, who have indeed a fatherly affection for them all, and who gladly make Our own.

It is indeed sad and incomprehensible that a man of Pius XI's stature could pen a document such as *Lux Veritatis*, containing as it does, such glaring errors and unfounded assumptions. Especially when his main

60 Mansi, IV, 1287.

points are flatly contradicted by some of the Catholic Church's finest historians e.g. Bossuet, Maret and Duchesne.

THE FOURTH ECUMENICAL COUNCIL

The Council of Chalcedon 451 A.D. (The Fourth Ecumenical Council) was called by the Emperor Marcian on the 17th of May in 451, to deal with the heresy of the Monophysites who held that in Christ there was only one nature - divine. This Council was summoned against the express wishes of Pope Leo, who only reluctantly agreed to it after the Emperor Marcian had convoked the Council. Pope Leo had, "begged the Emperor to defer the holding of the synod to a more peaceful time."[61] On another occasion Leo pleaded with the Emperor for a general council to be held in Italy, "..I entreat your clemency with groans and tears"[62] – the Emperor was unmoved. It is this Council of Chalcedon that Catholics will usually point to as evidence of Rome's supremacy being recognized by an ecumenical council, when the council fathers in accepting Pope St. Leo's Tome, - which insisted upon the two natures of Christ - cried out, "Peter has spoken through Leo". At first glance, this looks like a pretty good argument until we read the complete text:

---

61 Epistle ad Marcianum Augustum, S.Leo M. Ep. Ixxxiii.; P.L. liv. 920.

62 Epistle ad Theodosium Augustum, S. Leo M. Ep. xIiv. 6; P.L. liv. 829

> After reading of the foregoing epistle (Pope Leo's Tome), the most reverend bishops cried out: 'This is the faith of the fathers, this is the faith of the Apostles. So we all believe, thus the orthodox believe. Anathema to him does not thus believe. Peter has spoken thus through Leo. So taught the Apostles. Piously and truly did Leo teach, so taught Cyril. Everlasting be the memory of Cyril. Leo and Cyril taught the same thing, anathema to him who does not so believe. This is the true faith. Those of us who are orthodox thus believe'.

So we see Pope St. Leo and Cyril on equal footing in proclaiming the true faith. When we read the minutes of the council, we find that the Illyrian bishops thought St. Cyril's writings to be the benchmark of orthodoxy rather than Pope St. Leo's. In fact, in the 5th session they thought that Pope St. Leo had Nestorian leanings when they shouted, "The opponents are Nestorian, let them go to Rome!".[63] Note: the Church Fathers scrutinized Leo's tome before they declared it orthodox. They did not just accept it because it came from the Bishop of Rome. They were the ones empowered to declare what was orthodox, not the Bishop of Rome alone. As further proof against the church recognizing Rome's supreme jurisdiction, we only have to read canon 28 of this great council:

---

63 Imperial Unity and Christian Division, page 156, John Meyendorff, St. Vladimir's Seminary Press, Crestwood, New York, 1989.

> .....we also do enact and decree the same things concerning the privileges of the most holy Church of Constantinople, which is New Rome. For the Fathers rightly granted privileges to the throne of old Rome, because it was the royal city. And the One Hundred and Fifty most religious Bishops, actuated by the same consideration, gave equal privileges (<greek>isa<greek>presbeia<greek>) to the most holy throne of New Rome, justly judging that the city which is honoured with the Sovereignty and the Senate, and enjoys equal privileges with the old imperial Rome, should in ecclesiastical matters also be magnified as she is, and rank next after her, so that, in the Pontic, the Asian, and the Thracian dioceses, the metropolitans only and such bishops also of the Dioceses aforesaid as are among the barbarians, should be ordained by the aforesaid most holy throne of the most holy Church of Constantinople; every metropolitan of the aforesaid dioceses, together with the bishops of his province, ordaining his own provincial bishops, as has been declared by the divine canons; but that, as has been above said, the metropolitans of the aforesaid Dioceses should be ordained by the archbishop of Constantinople, after the proper elections have been held according to custom and have been reported to him.

Thus the council recognizes Rome's primacy of honour, but this recognition is political, i.e.. it was the ancient seat of Roman government - not theological. Thus rejecting Leo's vision of Rome's Primacy being based on a Divinely created "chair" of St. Peter.

Furthermore, this canon recalls that Rome's Primacy was granted by the Fathers of the Council of Nicea (Canon 6) - not by divine right. Pope St. Leo himself recognizes this when venting his displeasure to the Empress Pulcheria Augusta, at the idea of Constantinople enjoying equal status with Rome, he appeals not to Matthew 16:18 but to canon 6 of the Council of Nicea:

> For no one may venture upon anything in opposition to the enactments of the Fathers canons which many long years ago in the city of Nicea were founded upon the decrees of the Spirit, so that anyone who wishes to pass any different decree injures himself rather than impairs them.[64]

Pope Leo XIII boldly asserts in his encyclical *Satis Cognitum*: "The 28th Canon of the Council of Chalcedon, by the very fact that it lacks the assent and approval of the Apostolic See, is admitted by all to be worthless". The accuracy of this sweeping statement is in glaring contrast to history. In terms of the style of the time the Patriarch of Constantinople and the Emperor Marcian wrote conciliatory letters to Pope Leo, full of flattery and honeyed words, reminding him that Canon 28 "merely sanctioned a custom of 60 to 70 years in the dioceses of Pontus, Asia and Thrace".[65] The Patriarch

---

64 Nicene and Post Nicene Fathers of the Christian Church - Second Series, Volume XII, Leo the Great, Letter CV, Philip Schaff and Henry Wace, Wm. B. Eerdmans Publishing Company, Grand Rapids, Michigan.

65 Leo Donald Davis, page 192.

of Constantinople continued to exercise the jurisdictional power the canon invested him with and the Eastern Church, formally received this canon into its official canonical collection at the Council in Trullo in 690.[66]

THE FIFTH ECUMENICAL COUNCIL AND THE VACILLATIONS OF POPE VIGILIUS

Despite its condemnation by the Council of Ephesus, Nestorianism was still very much alive as were the Monophysites who were condemned by the Council of Chalcedon. Both these heretical groups bitterly opposed each other. Resolving this conflict and restoring peace was the challenge facing the Emperor Justinian. He was an ambitious, abstemious workaholic, with a gift for meticulous planning combined with endless patience. His faint, enigmatic smile is preserved in mosaic in the Church of St. Vitalea, Ravenna. His wife the stunningly beautiful Theodora, attracts more interest, being an ex prostitute and daughter of a circus bear keeper. There were times in Justinian's career when his courage failed him at a critical moment, however Theodora always stood by him cool and resolute. Justinian was devoted to her.

The Emperor Justinian thought he found a way of restoring unity in his empire by condemning the so-called *Three Chapters* in an Imperial Edict. These *Three Chapters*, were texts written by three fifth century

---

66 Ibid., page 194.

bishops, Theodore, Theodoret and Ibas, who were suspected of having Nestorian tendencies, however; all three had been cleared by the Council of Chalcedon But the exoneration of these men by a general council of the Church did not deter Justinian, because by doing this he thought he could win over the more moderate Monophysites. In 543-44 A.D., the Imperial condemnation was sent to the five leading Sees and under pressure four of the patriarchs signed, while Pope Vigilius procrastinated. Therefore, on the 22nd of November 545 A.D., an officer of the imperial guard sailed down the Tiber with an escort and seized the obstinate pope while he was celebrating mass at St. Cecilia in Rome and carried him off to Constantinople where he was to remain basically under house arrest for the next ten years.

Upon his arrival in Constantinople Vigilius refused to condemn the *Three Chapters* and refused to enter into communion with Mennas, Patriarch of Constantinople and others who had subscribed to the Imperial Edict. The following year in 548 A.D. however, Vigilius completely reversed his position and issued a document known as the *Judicatum* in which he formally anathematized the *Three Chapters*. In this action he was seen as betraying the Council of Chalcedon and a storm of protest followed. The West deserted him, including his own deacons in Rome and a council in North Africa led by Reparatus of Carthage excommunicated him. The British historian Judith Herrin draws the conclusion that this massive opposition, "sprang from a fundamental support for the oecumenical council as the highest authority within the church. Thus, they were not prepared to see the decisions of Chalcedon declared unorthodox".[67]

While Pope Vigilius caved in to this opposition and withdrew his *Judicatum* he secretly assured the Emperor Justinian by letter that he would do his utmost to procure the desired condemnation. Later however, Pope Vigilius again changed his mind and refused outright condemnation of the *Three Chapters*. By this time an exasperated Justinian summoned a council against Pope Vigilius' wishes,[68] which met in Constantinople on May 4th, 553 A.D. (this became the 5th Ecumenical Council). While the Council was in session Vigilius drew up his *Constitutum* in which he reverses his judgment for the third time. It could be argued that his *Judicatum* was written under duress, however; no such case could be made for the writing of this document, "which probably represented his true belief."[69] In his *Constitutum* the Pope condemns certain writings of Theodore but not his person and defends Theodoret and Ibas as being orthodox.[70] "Concerning the letter of Ibas, he wrote the following, that, 'understood in the best and most pious sense,' it was blameless."[71] He closes his encyclical with a solemn warning:

---

67 The Foundation of Christendom - page 121, Judith Herrin, Princeton University Press, Princeton, New Jersey, 1987.

68 Conciliar, Tom., v., col., 419., Labbe and Cossart.

69 The Popes, page 84, Vol. 1, edited by Eric John, Hawthorn Books Inc., New York, 1964.

70 Ibid., page 84.

71 Bossuet, Lib.,vij.,cap., xix..

> We ordain and decree that it be permitted to no one belonging to any ecclesiastical order or office to write or bring forward or compose or teach anything contrary to the contents of this *Constitutum* in regard to the Three Chapters, or after this present definition to move any further question. And if anything has been done said or written by anyone anywhere about the Three Chapters contrary to what we here assert and decree….. this in all ways we refute by the authority of the Apostolic See in which by the grace of God we preside.[72]

Pope Vigilius' *Constitutum* was a solemn judgment on faith and dogma, containing 61 anathemas issued by the Bishop of Rome to the Emperor and a General Council of the Church for their guidance and instruction. The finality of the judgment is exemplified by the words "ordain and decree". If this is not an *ex cathedra* statement what could it possibly be?

The Emperor Justinian, while refusing to receive Vigilius' *Constitutum* returned it with a scornful answer: "If you have in this condemned the *Three Chapters* I have no need of this new document, for I have from you many others of the same content. If, however, you have in this new document departed from your earlier declarations you have condemned yourself."[73] However, the 5th Ecumenical Council proceeded to pronounce its own judgment and condemned and anathematized the *Three Chapters* declaring

[72] Patrologiae Latinae Cursus Completus, 69: 112, J.P. Migne, Ed., Paris, 1844 - 66.

[73] Mansi, IX, 349.

furthermore, "We therefore anathematize….. those who have written or do write in defense of them, or who dare to say that they are correct, and who have defended or attempt to defend their impiety."[74] Obviously Vigilius fell under these anathemas of the Council and the Council ordered the Pope's name to be struck from the Diptychs of the Church, "on account of the impiety he defended."[75] The diptychs were the recognized symbol of unity, consisting of lists which each Patriarch kept in the churches of his jurisdiction, in order that prayers may be offered during the Liturgy for Patriarchs past and present whom he was in communion with. At the election of a new Patriarch, his fellow Patriarchs in the form of a Systatic Letter required a declaration of faith.

After six months, Pope Vigilius capitulated and reversed his judgment for a fourth time by issuing a second *Constitutum* dated 24th February 554 A.D., condemning and anathematizing the *Three Chapters* and blaming the devil for misleading him.[76] Thus the French Catholic Bishop Bossuet observed:

> These things prove, that in a matter of the utmost importance, disturbing the whole Church, and seeming to belong to the Faith, the decrees of sacred council prevail over the decrees of Pontiffs, and the letter Ibas, though defended by a judgment of the

74 Nicene and Post Nicene Fathers of the Christian Church, Second Series, Vol. XIV, The Seven Ecumenical Councils, page 311, Philip Schaff, D.D., LL.D. and Henry Wace, D. D., Wm. B. Eerdmans Publishing Company, Grand Rapids, Michigan. 1971.

75 Ibid., page 305.

76 The Popes, page 84.

Roman Pontiff could nevertheless be proscribed as heretical.[77]

THE SIXTH ECUMENICAL COUNCIL AND THE FALL OF POPE HONORIUS

A further humiliation awaited Rome with the 6th Ecumenical Council which was summoned by the Emperor Constantine IV in 680 A.D. at Constantinople to condemn the Monothelites. Monothelitism held that in Christ there was only one will - divine, rather than the orthodox formula, which calls for two wills, i.e. human and divine. One of the big proponents of Monothelitism, or single will, was Patriarch Sergius of Constantinople who, in order to gain support for his formula, sought the support of Pope Honorius. Pope Honorius responded in two letters that he accepted the idea that Christ had only one will: "we confess one will of our Lord Jesus Christ", (*unam voluntatem fatemur Domini nostri Jesu Christi*).[78] Honorius ends his letter, "These things your fraternity will preach with us, as we ourselves preach them like minded with you".[79]

Pope Honorius, Patriarch Sergius and others were anathematized as heretics by the 6th Ecumenical Council "we altogether reject them and execrate them as soul destroying and we have judged that the very names of those whose impious doctrines we execrate should be

---

77 Bossuet, *Def. Cleri Gall.,* Lib. Vij., cap. xix Abridged. Translation by Allies.

78 Mansi, XI, 539.

79 Ibid., XI, 545.

cast out of the Holy Church of God.....With them also we have judged that Honorius who was Pope of elder Rome, should be together with them cast out of the Holy Church of God, and be anathematized together with them because we have found from the letter written by him to Sergius that in all things he followed his own mind and confirmed his impious dogmas".[80] The Council then exclaimed; "Anathema to the heretic Sergius! Anathema to the heretic Honorius![81] The Council concluded by listing, "Honorius who was Pope of ancient Rome" among the instruments of the Devil.[82] The Emperor Constantine confirmed the Council's decrees stating: "We anathematize and reject those also who are the heretical promoters and patrons of the superfluous and new dogmas." Among these, "Honorius, who was Pope of elder Rome, who in all things promoted and cooperated with and confirmed their heresy".[83]

Pope Leo II confirmed the Council's decree on Rome's behalf in a letter to the Emperor: "Honorius, who did not attempt to sanctify this apostolic Church with the teaching of apostolical tradition but by profane treachery tried to subvert its spotless faith."[84] Lamenting to the Spanish bishops Pope Leo writes: "those who had been traitors against the purity of apostolical traditions, those who are gone, have been punished with eternal condemnation, that is

80 Ibid., XI, 553, 556.
81 Ibid., XI, 621.
82 Ibid., XI, 636.
83 Ibid., XI, 710.
84 Ibid., XI, 731.

Theodore.....with Honorius who did not extinguish the flame of heretical dogma but fanned it by his negligence."[85] To the Spanish king Pope Leo, while casting Honorius in the same company of heretics as Arius, Apollinarius, Nestorius etc., says: "Together with them Honorius, Bishop of Rome, who consented that the immaculate rule of apostolical tradition which he had received from his predecessors, should be polluted."[86] This condemnation of Pope Honorius was reaffirmed by the 7th Ecumenical Council in 787 and the 4th Council of Constantinople 868-870 and repeated by subsequent popes - over 50 from the 8th to the 11th century - at their elevation, since they had to confess and swear to uphold the decrees of the Ecumenical Councils. These oaths are contained in the *Liber Diurnus*, a book of oaths taken by the popes at their elevation during the early Middle Ages.[87] Until it was removed in the 16th century, the condemnation of Pope Honorius was commemorated in the *Roman Breviary* in the 3rd Lesson for the Feast of St. Leo, June 28th, it read: "St. Leo II.....accepted the Holy Sixth Council, wherein were condemned Cyrus, Sergius, Honorius, Pyrrhus.....who asserted or preached one will and operation in Our Lord Jesus Christ.....". [88] Ultimately references such as *Liber Diurnus* and the *Roman*

85 Ibid., XI, 1052.
86 Ibid., XI, 1057.
87 Liber Diurnus Romanorum Pontificum, V84. C65. A60. Gesamtausgabe, von Hans Foerster, Franke Verlag, Bern.
88 Papal Infallibility, page 51, G.G. Coulton, Litt. D., D. Litt., LL.D., F.B.A. Fellow of St. John's and Hon. Fellow of St. Catharine"s College, Cambridge. The Faith Press, Ltd. London, 1932.

Breviary that recorded the condemnation of a pope for heresy, came to be an embarrassment and their removal is recorded by Bishop Bossuet:

> The condemnation of Honorius .....exists in the *Liber Diurnus* seen and known by learned men for a long time passed. P. Garnier, a learned man of the utmost integrity of the Society of Jesus, Professor of Theology, has published it from the best manuscripts. It was also accustomed to be read in the life of St. Leo in the ancient Roman Breviaries down to our own time. But that *Diurnus* they suppress as far as lies in their power, and in the Roman Breviary they have erased these things. But are they therefore hidden? On all sides the truth breaks forth, and these things by so much the more appear as they are the more eagerly erased..... A cause is clearly lamentable which needs to be defended by such figments.[89]

The figure of a Pope being anathematized for heresy by an ecumenical council and his successors obviously presented difficulties for the doctrine of Papal Infallibility at the Vatican Council of 1870. There were those at the council who denied that Honorius had ever been condemned as a heretic, among them Archbishop Manning of England who stated that the two letters of Honorius, "are entirely orthodox" and that he was only "censured" for, "omission of apostolic authority".[90]

---

89 Bossuet, pars. iii. lib. vii., cxxvi, cap. ii, pages 45, 46. Lugani, 1766.

90 Petri Privelgium, page 223.

Dom Cuthbert Butler in his book *The Vatican Council 1869-1870,* quotes historian Abbot Chapman in putting to rest any doubt about Pope Honorius being condemned for heresy by the 6th Ecumenical Council:

> The attitude of the Ultramontane apologists and controversialists at the time of the Council was to question the authenticity of the documents, or to defend the substantial orthodoxy of Honorius' letters. Abbot Chapman says that both these positions should be abandoned: 'the authenticity of the documents is above suspicion'; and, in the face of the decree of the 6th Ecumenical Council and of divers papal acts, 'unquestionably no Catholic has the right to deny that Honorius was a heretic (though in the sense that Origen and Theodore Mopsuestia were heretics), a heretic in words, if not in intention'. 'It would no doubt be uncharitable to regard the Pope as a "private heretic": but his letters treated as definitions of faith, are obviously and beyond doubt heretical, for in a definition it is the words that matter'.[91]

It was claimed that Pope Honorius was not speaking *ex cathedra*, that is in his official teaching capacity because he only responded privately to Patriarch Sergius. However, the Patriarch of Constantinople was not interested in the private opinion of a Roman cleric named Honorius. He was formally asking Pope Honorius to render a verdict in his official capacity as

---

91 The Vatican Council 1869 - 1870, page 370, Dom Cuthbert Butler, Collins and Harvill Press, London, 1962.

Bishop of Rome, on a major controversy that was engulfing the Church at the time. The 6th Ecumenical Council stressed in its condemnation that Patriarch Sergius' first letter to Pope Honorius was "dogmatic" and that Honorius' reply was in kind.

THE SEVENTH ECUMENICAL COUNCIL

The decrees of this last ecumenical council clearly show that Rome's claims to supreme jurisdiction were still not completely recognized in the west. The Seventh Ecumenical Council (Nicea II) was called by the Empress Irene in 787 A.D. to affirm the veneration of icons against those who held that such veneration was idolatry - Iconoclasts. The decisions of this council affirming the veneration of icons, reached Charlemagne, King of the Franks in a very poor Latin translation and this barely literate German king rejected it. Pope Hadrian responded by defending the council, but Charlemagne ignored the Pope, whom he did not feel subordinate to in church affairs. He had a declaration issued called the *Libri Carolini,* which not only attacked the Second Council of Nicea and its affirmation of the use of sacred images, but also complained that in spite of the papal legates in attendance at the council, the Frankish Church was not represented.[92]

The *Libri Carolini* reserved its bitterest remarks for the Greeks, for whom Charlemagne had no liking and also for the Empress Irene, because he could not stand

92 Leo Donald Davis, S. J., page 312.

the idea of a female ruler: "for the weakness of her sex and her instability of mind forbids that she should hold the leadership over men in teaching and preaching".[93] Charlemagne called his own council in 794 A. D. (the Council of Frankfurt) to deal with the Spanish heresy and to repudiate the dogmatic decrees of the Second Council of Nicea - it was well attended as bishops came from the entire Western Church and upheld Charlemagne's repudiation. Despite Rome's formal acceptance, it took a long time before the Western Church recognized the Seventh Ecumenical Council (Nicaea II) e.g. even in the 9th century, despite his predecessors ratification and defense of the Seventh Ecumenical Council, Pope Nicholas I still only recognized the first six ecumenical councils as did France as late as the 11th century.[94]

As a final comment on the role of the papacy in the councils, we turn again to the British historian Judith Herrin who states that: "As few bishops of Rome had bilingual skills, they were increasingly dependent on Latin translations of Greek theological texts. Although canon law was recognized as fundamental to a universal faith, Rome had no complete Latin version of the decisions of the first four oecumenical councils until the sixth century. Full participation in the process of defining dogma and establishing ecclesiastical discipline was therefore denied to the See of St. Peter, for without

---

93 Ibid., page 312.

94 Encyclopedia Britannica - page 636, volume 6, 1972.

a complete knowledge of past rulings it was powerless."[95]

THE CROWNING OF CHARLEMAGNE AND THE OATH OF POPE HORMISDAS

Some Roman Catholics might point to the fact that Charlemagne was crowned as Holy Roman Emperor by Pope Leo III on Christmas morning in the year 800 A.D. and that this act surely suggests recognition of papal supremacy. Not really, as Norman F. Cantor explains in his book, *The Civilization of the Middle Ages*, Pope Leo III had been charged by the Roman nobility of "moral turpitude" and appealed to Charlemagne for help and protection. Charlemagne sent the pope to Rome under guard and "kept him in protective custody" until his trial on December 23, where under oath he had to clear himself of all accusations before Charlemagne - a dreadful humiliation for the papacy. Professor Norman F. Cantor describes the coronation through the eyes of Charlemagne's clerical biographer and secretary Einhard:

> On Christmas day 800, as Charlemagne rose from prayer before the tomb of St. Peter, Pope Leo suddenly placed the crown on the king's head, and the well-rehearsed Roman clergy and people shouted, 'Charles Augustus, crowned great and peace-giving emperor of the Romans, life and victory!' Charlemagne was so indignant and

[95] Judith Herrin, Pages 104 - 105.

chagrined that, according to Einhard, 'he said he would never have entered the church on that day, although it was a very important religious festival, if he had known the intention of the pope'.[96]

In describing this same scene British Byzantine scholar John Julius Norwich writes:

But if Leo conferred a great honour on Charles that Christmas morning, he bestowed a still greater one on himself: the right to appoint, and to invest with crown and scepter, the Emperor of the Romans. Here was something new, perhaps even revolutionary. No Pontiff had ever before claimed for himself such a privilege - not only establishing the imperial crown as his own personal gift but simultaneously granting himself implicit superiority over the Emperor whom he had created.[97]

John Julius Norwich and other historians claim that Pope Leo III derived his authority for this incredible act, from the forged Donation of Constantine - a document we will discuss in Chapter V. In 813 at Aarchen, it was not the pope but Charlemagne who crowned his son Louis emperor.

Many Catholic historians claim that the Eastern Churches have always recognized the supreme

---

96 Civilization of the Middle Ages - page 181, Norman F. Cantor, Harper Perennial, New York, 1993.

97 Byzantium, The Early Centuries - page 379, John Julius Norwich, Viking, London, 1988.

jurisdiction of Rome and they usually point to the Oath of Pope Hormisdas. The Acacian schism had divided the Eastern and Western Church for 35 years and upon his ascension to the throne in 518 A.D., the Emperor Justin decided he was going to rule over one empire and one church and entrusted his nephew Justinian, with the task of ending the schism.

To accomplish this, Justinian needed the support of the Bishop of Rome. Being in a strong bargaining position, Pope Hormisdas placed a very high price for reconciliation, i.e. wholesale excommunications, including the Patriarchs Euphemius and Macedonius, who according to Byzantine scholar John Julius Norwich…., "had never veered from the orthodox path and had indeed suffered exile for their beliefs….."[98] Last and certainly not least, was the following oath that each bishop was to sign:

> In following in all things the apostolic see and in professing all its constitutions, I hope that I will deserve to remain in the same communion with you which is professed by the apostolic see, in which persists the total and true strength of the Christian religion. Promising also not to recite in the liturgy the names of men who have been separated from communion with the Catholic Church which means, who do not agree with the apostolic see…..[99]

---

98 Ibid., - page 191.

99 Cambridge Medieval History, Vol. 2, pages 246 - 247, Cambridge at the University Press, 1967..

Justinian accepted Pope Hormisdas' conditions and using imperial authority forced the Eastern Church to comply. Before signing the document, John Patriarch of Constantinople added the following sentence: "I hold the most holy Church of the old and the new Rome to be one. I define the see of the Apostle Peter and this of the imperial city to be one see."[100] In doing this, he was recalling the fact that canon 28 of the Council of Chalcedon declared that the Sees of Rome and Constantinople were equal. "The cost, from the Byzantine point of view, had been an almost unconditional surrender, involving the sacrifice of two innocent reputations; but to Justinian it was a small enough price to pay for a reunited Church".[101] It was this same Justinian as emperor, who we saw earlier bringing Pope Vigilius to Constantinople and placing him under house arrest for ten years, in order to gain his acceptance of another formula, which would secure a unified church within his empire.

British Byzantine scholar, Sir Steven Runciman flatly rejects the claim that the Eastern Church had always recognized the claims of the papacy:

> The Emperors considered the Pope to be their subject as well as the Patriarch; and the Pope was more important because he was physically less easy to control and politically more useful owing to the influence that he commanded in Italy. Thus if the Pope could be placated by humiliating the Patriarch,

---

100 Meyendorff, page 214..

101 John Julius Norwich., page 191.

> the Emperor was usually prepared to order the Patriarch to recognize papal superiority, and was himself anxious to show deference to the Pope's office. . . . Thus if some eleven Patriarchs of Constantinople admitted the superiority of the Pope, they made the admission at the Emperors bidding, and their successors felt themselves at liberty to consider them wrong in doing so.[102]

Harvard University's Roman Catholic Byzantine scholar Francis Dvornik's view is consistent with that of Sir Steven Runciman's when he writes:

> But their fear of compromising the autonomy of their Churches prevented the Orientals from accepting the claims that were made by certain Popes, especially Gelasius, Symmacus and Nicholas I, the claim to direct and immediate jurisdiction over the whole Church, including the East. [103]

The Eastern Church vigorously defended the principles of collegiality, which they saw as the true and traditional form of church government, against the rising monarchical concept of church government advanced by the papacy. The two models of church government were obviously mutually exclusive and it

---

102 Runciman, page 18.

103 Byzantium and the Roman Primacy, page 165, Francis Dvornik, Fordham University Press, 1966.

was only a matter of time before east and west went their respective ways.

CHAPTER IV

Filioque and the Schism

As far back as I can remember when discussing church history with friends, I can still hear myself saying, "but the Orthodox are right on Filioque". In fairness I had to acknowledge that they had a point. Filioque refers to the inclusion into the Nicene-Constantinopolitan Creed that the Holy Spirit proceeds from the Father and the Son - in Latin, Filioque. The unity of the one undivided Holy Catholic Church was expressed in the celebration of the Eucharist and in the recitation of the Creed - a declaration of faith confessed by the entire Church. For any part of the church to change the Creed without benefit of an Ecumenical Council, would be to create enormous divisions.

In tracing this controversy both Catholic and Non-Catholic scholars agree on the following. The Creed of the Church, the so called Nicene Creed, was hammered out at the First and Second Ecumenical Councils, (First Council of Nicea 325 A.D. and the First Council of Constantinople 381 A.D.) - it read that the Holy Spirit proceeds from the Father - not the Father and the Son (Filioque). The Third and Fourth Ecumenical Councils, (Ephesus 431 A.D and Chalcedon 451 A.D.) specifically prohibited any changes to the Creed.

It is interesting that the insertion of Filioque in the Creed, "done so casually and almost inadvertently", made its first appearance at the National Council of

Toledo, Spain, in 589 A.D. - "a country which was then rather peripheral in the Christian world"[104], and from there spread throughout the Western Church. It is also interesting to note, that the Spanish Church felt itself autonomous enough to reject the Fifth Ecumenical Council of 553 A.D.[105] and reaffirm the Filioque insertion at subsequent councils in Toledo in 633 A.D. and 653 A.D.[106]

Rome resisted this innovation and defended the Creed as laid down by the Ecumenical Councils. Even as late as 879-880 A.D., Pope John VIII, through his legates at the Council of Constantinople, reaffirmed Rome's opposition to its use. Also Pope Leo III 795-816 A.D., while not personally seeing anything wrong with the Filioque clause, forbade its use on the grounds that the Ecumenical Councils had forbidden any additions to be made to the Creed. To reinforce his defense of the original Creed, he had two silver plaques, one in Latin and one in Greek, placed before the tomb of St. Peter containing the Creed without the Filioque.[107] However, in violation of the Pope's commands, Filioque continued to be used in the court of Charlemagne and throughout the West. Eventually, around 1014 Rome accepted it into her liturgy. On these points both Catholic and non-Catholic scholars agree.

---

104 The Formation of Christendom, page 230, Judith Herrin, Princeton University Press, Princeton, New Jersey.

105 Ibid., page 239.

106 Byzantium and the Roman Papacy, page 13, Francis Dvornik, Fordham University Press, 1966.

107 Encyclopedia of Early Christianity, Garland Publishing Inc., New York and London, 1990.

The question of course, is why did Rome after resisting Filioque for 500 years, sanction its use? The answer of most scholars is the most obvious one - it was too firmly entrenched in the West and therefore Rome capitulated, as she did with forbidden practices that were too firmly entrenched in our own day, e.g. communion in the hand, altar girls and liturgical dance. Sir Steven Runciman, the British Byzantine scholar gives the Eastern prospective on the Filioque dispute:

> But behind the theological issue lay another about which the East felt even more strongly. The Creed had been issued by an Oecumenical Council, which was in Eastern eyes the one inspired doctrinal authority. To add to the Creed was to question the authority and inspiration of the Fathers of the Church. Only another Oecumenical Council had the right, not indeed to alter, but to amplify and explain the decisions reached at an earlier council. If the Western Churches tampered unilaterally with the Creed of the councils they must thereby automatically lapse into heresy; nor would any pronouncement by the Pope in their favour serve to condone them. The East saw in the dispute a direct attack on its whole theory of Church government and doctrine.[108]

Within a very short space of time after Rome's adoption of Filioque, the Eastern Christians were called heretics by their Western brethren for denying it. For

---

108 The Eastern Schism, page 32, Steven Runciman, Oxford University Press, 1956.

the Orthodox, Filioque obscures our understanding of the Trinity which is the central core of our Christian faith. The Orthodox derive their understanding of this position from the Gospel of St. John 15:26, "But when the Paraclete cometh, whom I will send you from the Father, the Spirit of truth who proceedeth from the Father, He shall give testimony of Me." Also the Gospel of St. John 14:16, "And I will ask the Father, and he shall give you another Paraclete, that He may abide with you forever" and again the Gospel of St. John 14:26, "But the Paraclete, the Holy Ghost, whom the Father will send in my name, he will teach you all things, and bring all things to your mind, whatsoever I shall have said to you".

Here the Bible tells us from the words of Christ, that the Holy Spirit proceeds from the Father alone and it is this understanding that forms the basis of the original Nicene Creed i.e., that there are three well defined Persons in one God. The insertion of Filioque the Orthodox assert, destroys the distinct personhood between the Father, Son and Holy Spirit in the Trinity, thus fusing the Father and Son into one and subordinating the Holy Spirit in this relationship. This the Orthodox argue, hints of Sabellianism. Sabellius was a second century heretic who taught that the Son and Holy Spirit were only names signifying one indistinct Godhead.

The Eastern Fathers stressed the distinctive personhood of the Father, Son and Holy Spirit within the Trinity and from this point advanced to the divine being or essence. In the West the Fathers inverted this process, stressing the unity of the divine being or essence within the Trinity and then advancing towards distinct personhood. Some Orthodox theologians have stated that the centralized, authoritarian, papal structure in the Western Church, has its origins in its Trinitarian theology, which stresses the unity of the Godhead at the expense of the diversity or distinctive personhood of the Trinity.[109]

The Roman Catholic response is that the Filioque insertion was not advancing another belief, but merely expressing in a different way the same truth and that both formulas are thoroughly compatible. The Orthodox reply to this, is that the Creed belongs to the entire Church and one part of the Church does not have the right to change it, without the consent of all. Ecumenical councils produced the Creed and ecumenical councils prohibited any changes. Rome was party to all of this; therefore, if Rome wishes to make a change in the Creed then an ecumenical council is the only competent body to deal with it. In recent years Pope John XXIII and more recently Pope John Paul II, have in joint celebrations with Orthodox dignitaries, recited the Creed without the Filioque insertion. Today, in an attempt to understand each other's position, there is an ongoing dialogue between Orthodox and Roman Catholic theologians on the Filioque interpolation in the Creed.

---

109 The Orthodox Church, New addition, page 216, Timothy Ware, Penguin Books.

CHAPTER IV

MUTUAL INCOMPREHENSION - THE SACK OF CONSTANTINOPLE - SCHISM

The year 1054 is usually given as the date for the schism between the two great branches of the Christian church. However, this neat clear-cut; one could almost say surgical separation, as if they were in communion one day and not the next, is a vast oversimplification. Relations between the two great churches of Rome and Constantinople, had been slowly deteriorating long before the 11th century over issues of Filioque and papal claims. Even after 1054, communications still flowed between the two great Sees.

A more sure date for the final separation between the two great churches, would be April 12th, 1204 when the 4th Crusade attacked and sacked Constantinople for 30 days, which Sir Steven Runciman describes as ….. "one of the most ghastly and tragic incidents in history ….. More immediately horrifying were the outrages committed on men, women and children of the city and on its priests, monks and nuns."[110] Every church was sacked and emptied, their great libraries were burnt to the ground destroying countless ancient manuscripts and works of art. Nicetas Choniates, Archbishop of Athens, echoed Eastern Christendom when he protested, "You took the Cross upon your shoulders; and on that Cross and on the Holy Gospels you swore that you would pass over Christian lands without violence….. Far from carrying the Cross you profane it and trample it under foot. You claim to be in quest of a pearl beyond price,

---

110 Runciman, pages 149 - 150.

but in truth you fling that most precious of all pearls, which is the body of our Saviour, into the mud. The Saracens themselves show less impiety."[111] The crusaders brought not peace but a sword and the sword was to sever Christendom. The separation of East and West was now complete.

It is still however, well worth relating the schism of 1054 because it highlights the differences and mutual incomprehension that had gradually developed between the two churches; especially the papal reforms which insisted on the recognition of Rome's demands for absolute authority over the entire church.

The spark that ignited the schism between Rome and Constantinople was the question of jurisdictional rights over the diocese in Byzantine territories in Southern Italy. These territories were held by Norman freebooters and with papal approval[112] were forcing the Greek Churches to adopt Latin practices such as using unleavened bread for the sacrament. When Michael Cerularius, Patriarch of Constantinople, heard this he immediately retaliated and ordered the Latin Churches in his jurisdiction to conform to Greek practices. Those who protested suffered closure.

Michael Cerularius then made a fateful error in judgment, he enlisted Leo, Archbishop of Ochrid, head of the Bulgarian Church in the writing of a letter to the Byzantine Bishop, John of Trani in Apulia. This letter

---

111 Nicetas Choniates, 'Alexius Ducas,' IV, iv.

112 a) Runciman, page 41 & b) Byzantium the Apogee, page 317, John Julius Norwich, Alfred A. Knopf, New York, 1992.

in which he vehemently attacked the practices of the Latin Church, such as the use of azymes (unleavened bread) etc., was to be passed on to the "most reverend Pope" and "all the bishops of the Franks". When Pope Leo IX read this vitriolic epistle, he was deeply offended and quickly responded in kind with a detailed document disrespectfully addressed, "to Michael of Constantinople and Leo of Ochrid, Bishops", in which he lectured them on the supremacy of Rome. The rationale for these papal claims was taken from the forged Donation of Constantine[113] - (for a full treatment on this document, see Chapter VI) - a document unknown to the Byzantines. Before this letter was sent two letters arrived, one from the Emperor and the other from Patriarch Michael Cerularius. The letter from the Emperor is lost, but the letter from Michael Cerularius, was considerate, friendly and while pointedly avoiding any reference to the disputed practices, prayed for closer ties between the Churches.

Pope Leo, still smarting from the first letter, angrily rejected this peaceful overture and drafted two letters, one to the Emperor and the other to Patriarch Michael Cerularius. In his letter to the Patriarch, he restated the claims of supreme jurisdiction for the See of Rome; scolded and reproved him for having the audacity of questioning Rome's judgment in her practices, for displaying vaulting ambition in using the title Ecumenical and in his final salvo he insultingly implied

113 a) The Papal Monarchy, The Western Church From 1050 to 1250, page 137, Colin Morris, Clarendon Press, Oxford, 1991, b) Runciman, page 42.

without any proof or justification, that his election as Patriarch had been uncanonical. The letter to the Emperor, while attacking the Patriarchs character, requested safe conduct for the legates bearing the letters. As his legates, Pope Leo chose Humbert of Mourmoutiers, Cardinal of Silva Candida, who headed the delegates, Cardinal Frederick of Lorraine, (later Pope Stephen IX) and Archbishop Peter of Amalfi.

In his selection of Cardinal Humbert, Pope Leo displayed poor judgment, for Humbert as we shall see, was a proud, vain man of mercurial temperament - totally unsuited to the task at hand. The Patriarch they were sent to meet was a man of uncompromising temperament, who was very sensitive about the dignity of his office. It was a recipe for disaster. The papal legates arrived in Constantinople in April 1054 and first called on the Patriarch. They felt that their reception by the Patriarch lacked the deference due to their rank and handing him the papal letter they turned on their heels and left. When Michael Cerularius opened the letter, he fumed not only at its contents, but also that his gesture of good will had been contemptuously ignored. Worse still, the seals of the letter appeared to have been tampered with - who else had read it? However, an even greater humiliation awaited the Patriarch.

Emboldened by the warm reception they received by the Emperor, the three papal legates had Pope Leo's first undelivered letter addressed to Patriarch Michael Cerularius - a letter whose existence he was totally ignorant of - translated into Greek and freely distributed in the city. This was the last straw. From here on the

Patriarch would refuse them any recognition. Pope Leo's circulated letter drew a response from Nicetas Stethatus a monk from the Studium Monastery. Addressed to the "Roman Church", it politely criticized Rome's insistence on a celibate priesthood, its use of unleavened bread and fasting on Saturdays. Upon reading it, Cardinal Humbert flew into a fury and issued a reply full of shrill invective, in which page after page he hurled abuse upon Nicetas Stethatus. Calling him a "pestiferious pimp" and a "disciple of the malignant Mahomet" and that he was more likely housed in a brothel than a monastery.

Meanwhile, Michael Cerilarius remained aloof and detached above the fray in his Patriarchal Palace, observing the crude boorish behaviour of the papal legates. The emperor however, could not share Cerilarius' detachment for fearing the loss of a much needed papal alliance he needed to regain his lost territories in Southern Italy, and therefore, forced Nicetas Stethatus to retract his letter and personally apologize to Humbert.

On April 15th, shortly after the legates arrived in Constantinople, Pope Leo died. When he heard the news, Michael Cerularius must have positively relished the expectant scene of the three papal legates packing their bags and returning from whence they came - and the sooner the better. Which is precisely what they should have done; by all the statutes of canon law, their legatine mission died with the pope who sent them. The fact that they were now without diplomatic standing, did not regrettably restrain their ability to give offense.

Emboldened by the Emperor's support in forcing the monk Stethatus to recant and apologize, Humbert raised the delicate issue of Filioque in the Creed with him - a subject the Byzantines were positively adamant on. Michael Cerularius continued to maintain his silence; completely ignoring their presence.

Humbert would endure the Patriarch's studied disregard no longer and at 3 o'clock in the afternoon of Saturday, July 16th, 1054, at the commencement of the Divine Liturgy, the three ex-legates marched into the great domed church of Hagia Sophia (Holy Wisdom) in full ecclesiastical regalia and laid their Bull of Excommunication on the high altar in the presence of the assembled clergy. They then strode out of the church, pausing only to shake the dust from their feet. A deacon ran after them clutching the bull, pleading with them to retract it. They refused his entreaties and the Bull was dropped in the street.

It was bad enough that these three individuals were without diplomatic standing and that therefore, their Bull violated canon law, but the contents of the Bull itself displayed an abysmal ignorance of the Eastern Church. Sir Steven Runciman comments:

> Few important documents have been so full of demonstrable errors. It is indeed extraordinary that a man of Humbert's learning could have penned so lamentable a manifesto. It began by refusing to Cerularius, both personally and as Bishop of Constantinople, the title of Patriarch. It declared that there was nothing to be said against the citizens

> of the Empire or of Constantinople, but that all those who supported Cerularius were guilty of simony (which, as Humbert well knew, was the dominant vice at the time of his own church), of encouraging castration (a practice that was also followed at Rome), of insisting on rebaptizing Latins (which, at that time was untrue), of allowing priests to marry (which was incorrect; a married man could become a priest but no one who was already ordained could marry), of baptizing women in labour, even if they were dying (a good Early Christian practice), of jettisoning the Mosaic Law (which was untrue), of refusing communion to men who had shaved their beards (which again was untrue, though the Greeks disapproved of shaven priests), and finally, of omitting a clause in the Creed (which was the exact reverse of the truth). After such accusations complaints about the closing of the Latin churches at Constantinople and of disobedience to the Papacy lost their effect. The final **anathema maranatha** was followed by a statement that henceforward Cerularius and his supporters would be known as Prozymite heretics.[114]

The three ex-legates departed for Rome two days later, laden with gifts from an Emperor who still sought a papal alliance. Once the contents of the Bull were made public, the people of Constantinople rose up in anger; there were riots and demonstrations throughout the city, with some of the fury directed at the Emperor himself, for being excessively hospitable to these

---

114 Runciman, page 48.

Roman offenders. Peace was only restored when the Bull of Excommunication was publicly burnt and the three offending ex-legates were excommunicated and anathematized. The document of excommunication was carefully worded so that it did not include the Papacy or the Western Church.

This is a sad story where both Rome and Constantinople can share some of the blame. But, as John Julius Norwich says; "The fatal blow was struck by the disempowered legates of a dead Pope, representing a headless Church - since the new Pontiff had not yet been elected - and using an instrument at once uncanonical and inaccurate."[115]

---

[115] Norwich, page 322.

CHAPTER V

The Gregorian Revolution

The Gregorian reforms of the 11th century signaled for the Western Church, a radical departure from the Church of the Seven Ecumenical Councils. This ancient collegial structure of church government, that offered a common forum for both churches east and west to settle differences and thus provide a common bond, was to be replaced in the west with a papal monarchy, exercising an authoritarian, highly centralized form of church government that ultimately controlled every aspect of church life. Through its new found claims of temporal power, the papacy would conduct wars, sign treaties, form alliances, depose kingdoms and would challenge Europe's concept of the divine right of kings. With these reforms Rome "substituted, perhaps fatally, visible organizational unity for the unity of love and mixed the kind of power represented by the Roman Empire with that of the Cross and the resurrection."[116]

Lying in the Northern reaches of central Italy, is the district of Emilia - Romagna, an area famous for its gastronomy, historical attractions and scenic beauty. Perched 1,890 feet above sea level in the Appennines, 12 miles south west of the city of Reggio nell Emilia, lie the ruins of the fortress of Canossa. It was here beneath

---

116 A History of Christianity, Vol. 1, page 340, Kenneth Scott Latourette, Harper Row, New York, Evenston, San Francisco, London.

the wind swept battlements of Canossa on January 25th, 1077, that Henry IV the German King knelt for three days in the snow (undoubtedly an exaggeration) as a penitent begging the forgiveness of Pope Gregory VII (Hildebrand) the vigorous reforming Pope.

It was one of the great scenes of European history; an anointed king publicly recognizing the unprecedented papal claims of temporal power. This was the high water mark of Gregory's series of reforms in which he wrested the Church from lay control. Lay rulers had the right to invest bishops and abbots in their offices, usually for a hefty fee, a. practice called simony; named after Simon Magus in the Book of Acts who attempted to purchase the gifts of the Holy Spirit. This feature of lay investiture was a cause of great scandal in the Western Church and starting with Gregory's predecessor Pope Leo IX, there was a concerted effort to regain control of the church.

Ending with the pontificate of John VIII in 882 (who was hammered to death), the papacy entered into a steep decline for 164 years. This period of spiritual and moral bankruptcy was undoubtedly the worst period in the history of the papacy. During this time the papacy fell under the control of the German Crown who appointed 21 out of 25 popes.[117] In 1046 the pious German Emperor Henry III, stung by the unedifying spectacle of three men simultaneously claiming the papal office, marched on Rome and deposed them. His choice of

---

[117] The Christian East and the Rise of the Papacy, page 29, Aristeides Papadakis, in collaboration with John Meyendorff, St. Vladimir's Seminary Press, Crestwood, New York 1994.

Suitger, Bishop of Bamberg (Clement II) was to be the first of a series of German Popes of high moral fiber who together with their Emperor were keen on reforming the Church.

The reform movement really got under way with the election of Pope Leo IX (1049-1054). His pontificate only lasted five years but, by the time of his death the character of Western Christendom had permanently changed. He convened 11 or 12 synods condemning simony and clerical marriage and reasserting the canonical election of bishops. To assure the future of the reform movement, Leo brought men of outstanding ability into the senior ranks of the clergy. These talented committed idealists would continue Leo's work long after his death.

Pope Leo IX was also the first Pope to personally wage war, when he conducted a disastrous campaign against the Normans which ended with him being taken prisoner (as we saw in Chapter IV). The spectacle of priests, bishops and monks bearing arms and shedding blood came as a shock to the Orthodox. "Typically, (Byzantine) priests who took up arms against the Arabs (and thus often shed blood) were either deposed or excommunicated by their episcopal superiors."[118] The Byzantine princess and diarist, Anna Comnena recorded her revulsion at the sight of armed clerics in the ranks of the crusaders.[119] In fact the very notion of warfare itself being considered holy, was one of the more radical ideas which the men of the reformed papacy introduced

---

118 Ibid., page 88.

119 Alexiad, X, 8, Anna Comnena, Leib, 2:218.

into Western Christianity - they "were the very men who stood for the idea of holy war and sought to put it into practice."[120]

The papacy of Gregory VII (Hildebrand) and Urban II, "saw the reversal of a thousand years of Christian tradition, when the Gregorian papacy accepted warfare without reservation as a meritorious activity and the profession of arms as a Christian vocation so long as it was directed toward the extirpation of what is alien to Christianity both inside and outside Christian society."[121] This is best exemplified by St. Bernard of Clairvaux in his work, *In Praise of the New Knighthood*, where he exhorts the crusaders that: "the knight of Christ need fear no sin in killing the foe, he is a minister of God for the punishment of the wicked. In the death of a pagan a Christian is glorified, because Christ is glorified."[122]

A REVOLUTION BREACHES ITS BOUNDARIES

Norman F. Cantor makes the point in his book, *The Civilization of the Middle Ages,* that world revolutions always have just grievances as an initial rallying point - the French and Russian Revolutions being a good example. The evils of lay investiture, resulting in simony and clerical corruption, was the rallying cry of the Gregorian reform and was to provide the basis of the

---

120 The Origin of the Idea of Crusade, page 143, Erdmann.
121 Holy War, page 27, T. P. Murphy, Ed, Columbus, OH, 1976.
122 De Laude Novae Militiae, Sancti Bernardi Opera, 3:217.

first great revolution in Western Society. The greatness of this revolution was not in its redressing of the evils of lay investiture; had it confined itself only to this it would have warranted no more than a few pages in a history book. What made this revolution great was that it did what all other great revolutions did; it quickly spread beyond the boundaries of its original grievances.

As Cantor points out, "the ultimate aim of the revolutionary ideologist has been not the reform of the prevailing system but its abolition and replacement by a new order."[123] The grievance of lay investiture was to provide the springboard for liberating the Church from state control, negating the "sacramental character of kingship" and elevating the papacy to an absolute monarchy with total authority over the Church and temporal rulers.

While it was the claim of temporal power, which historian Arnold Toynbee called, "the great Hildebrandine error", that gave the Gregorian revolution its greatness, it is precisely this claim that ultimately undermined the spiritual authority of the papacy. Resulting in the Great Schism and leaving, on the eve of the Protestant Revolt, a European people grown weary with the struggle between the papacy and kings, vowing to rule their own respective kingdoms free of outside interference.

The creed or manifesto for the Gregorian reform, is to be found in the Dictus Papae (Statements of the

---

123 The Civilization of the Middle Ages, page 245, Norman F. Cantor, Harper Perrenial, New York, 1994.

Pope), published by Gregory VII shortly after taking office:

1. That the Roman Church was founded by God alone.
2. That the Roman pontiff alone is rightly to be called universal.
3. That he alone can depose or reinstate bishops.
4. That his legate, even if of a lower grade, takes precedence, in a council, of all bishops and may render a sentence of deposition against them.
7. That for him alone it is lawful to enact new laws according to the needs of the time, to assemble together new congregations, to make an abbey or a canonry; and, on the other hand, to divide a rich bishopric and unite the poor ones.
8. That he alone may use the imperial insignia.
9. That the pope is the only one whose feet are to be kissed by all princes.
11. That his title is unique in the world.
12. That he may depose emperors.
16. That no synod may be called a general one without his order.
17. That no chapter or book may be regarded as canonical without his authority.
19. That he himself may be judged by no one.
21. That to this see the more important cases of every Church should be submitted.

22. That the Roman Church has never erred, nor ever, by the witness of Scripture, shall err to all eternity.
26. That he should not be considered as Catholic who is not in conformity with the Roman Church.[124]

The claims were breathtaking. Some of them would have been considered blasphemous by such Popes as St. Gregory the Great who wrote, "whosoever calls himself, or desires to be called, Universal Priest, is in his elation the precursor of Antichrist."[125] To the kings of Western Europe, seated in their castles and palaces, the gasps of amazement and incredulous anger would have been something to behold. Items 9 and 12 must have caused more than one monarch to choke on his mead. Further shocks awaited them when Gregory in a letter to Herman Bishop of Metz dated March 15th, 1081 (a letter widely distributed), instructed the crown heads of Europe:

> Who does not know that kings and princes derive their origin from men ignorant of God who raised themselves above their fellows by pride, plunder,

---

124 Das Register Gregors VII, Epistolae selectae 2:201 - 8, E. Caspar, Ed. English translation in S. Z. Ehler and J.B. Morrall, Church and State Through the Centuries, Westminster, M.D. 1954, 43 - 44.

125 Nicene and Post-NiceneFathers of the Christian Church, Edited by Philip Schaff, D.D., LL.D., and Henry Wace, D.D., Vol. X11, Leo the Great, Gregory the Great. Espitle XXXIII Pope St. Gregory to Mauricius Augustus. Wm. B. Eerdmans Publishing Company, Grand Rapids, Michigan.

> treachery, murder - in short, by every kind of crime - at the instigation of the Devil, the prince of this world, men blind with greed and intolerable in their audacity?[126]

In a letter to Bishop Altmann of Passau and Abbot William of Hirschau, dated March 10th, 1081, Gregory declares that kings will now be judged on their suitability and usefulness to Holy Church and under oath will serve the pope as their feudal lord:

> From this hour onward I will be the liegeman (*fidelis*) of the holy Apostle Peter and of his vicar Gregory now living. And whatever he shall command me with the words, "by (your) strict obedience," I will faithfully perform as befits a Christian man. As regards the regulation of churches and the lands or revenues given to St. Peter by the emperor Constantine and Charles, also all churches or estates granted to the Apostolic See by any man or woman at any time and which are or may be in my power, I will make such arrangements with the pope that I shall not incur the danger of sacrilege or imperil my soul. I will, with Christ's help, pay to God and St. Peter all due honour and service. And on the day when I shall first come into his (the pope's) presence I will faithfully give my hand as the vassal (*miles*) of him and of St. Peter.[127]

---

126 The Correspondence of Pope Gregory VII, Selected Letters from the Registrum, Translated by Ephraim Emerton, page 169, W. W. Norton & Company Inc., New York.'

127 Ibid., page 180.

Some of these claims had been made long ago by previous popes, but they had always remained distant and theoretical because no pope before had the will or the means to carry them out. Besides, for almost two hundred years the papacy had been a negligible entity. Pope Gregory had already tested these principles early in his pontificate in 1076, when the See of Milan became vacant.

The German King Henry IV opposed Gregory's candidate in favour of his own and in the face of Gregory's demands, sent a letter calling him a "false monk" and ordering him to vacate the chair of St. Peter. Gregory was not intimidated and he excommunicated the German king and informed the bishops and abbots that they too would suffer excommunication if they were to recognize Henry as their king. "Since at least two thirds of Henry's army came from ecclesiastical lands, he had lost the greater part of his military power without a blow being struck."[128] With the German princes and nobility already circling the growing power vacuum, Henry knew he had to act fast to save his crown. Quickly crossing the Alps, he encountered Pope Gregory at Canossa and made his famous act of penance.

---

128 Cantor, page 269.

CHAPTER V

"BUT THE FORGERS HAD CONSIDERABLE INFLUENCE"

The creation of a systematic code of canon law was to provide the basis on which the reformed papacy would strengthen its authority. What they currently had was inadequate, so the papal researchers had to sift through enormous quantities of material e.g. the writings of the Church Fathers, papal decretals, material from papal registers, documents from the councils, contradictory legal judgments etc.. Much of the material they drew on came from the False Decretals of Pseudo-Isidore - a collection of genuine and spurious material. They are called Pseudo-Isidore because the forgers attributed the collection to St. Isidore of Seville. They date from the 9th century and appear to have been used for the first time at the Council of Soissons in 835.

The first of this three- part collection is "completely spurious" containing 70 forged letters "attributed to Popes before the Council of Nicaea" (325 also included were "two spurious letters of Clement which were already in circulation". The majority of the second part of the collection containing the canons of Councils are genuine, the notable exception being the famous Donation of Constantine. The third collection contains a skillful blending of false and genuine decretals - "Blended thus of genuine and spurious matter".[129]

The aim of the False Decretals of Pseudo-Isidore was to create a centralized church with the Bishop of

[129] The Cambridge Medieval History, Vol. 5, page 711, Cambridge at the University Press, 1957.

Rome at its head exercising complete universal authority. They, "depicted the pope as claiming supreme authority from the beginning".[130] These forgeries claim for instance that Pope Anacletus (c.92-101), wrote that Christ through His apostles ordained that, "the greater and difficult questions must be referred always to the Apostolic See".[131] That St. Athanasius wrote to Pope Felix II (483-492), "The canons certainly enjoin that apart from the Roman Pontiff we must not decide anything about the greater causes..... For we know that in the great Nicene Synod" (Council of Nicea), "of three hundred and eighteen bishops it was unanimously enjoined that without the consent of the Roman Pontiff a Council could not be held nor a bishop be condemned."[132] The problem with this particular quote is two fold. First no Ecumenical Council ever passed such a resolution and secondly, the pontificate of Pope Felix II was from 483 to 492 while Athanasius lived from 297 to 373.

"But the forgers had a considerable influence"[133] in that the church was now being molded in a form that did not reflect its catholic tradition, but rather the bias of 9th century forgers.[134] The great 19th century Catholic layman and historian, Lord Acton wrote:

---

130 A History of Christianity, Vol. 1, page 342, Kenneth Scott Latourette, Harper San Francisco.

131 Decretals Pseudo-Isidorianae, page 73, Paulus Hinchius, Scientia Verlag Aalen, 1963.

132 Ibid., page 479.

133 Encyclopaedia Britannica, Vol. 7, page 163, 1972.

134 The Papal Monarchy, The Western Church from 1050 to 1250, page 31, Colin Morris, Clarendon Press, Oxford, 1991.

> Religious knowledge in those days suffered not only from ignorance and the defect of testimony, but from an excess of fiction and falsification. Whenever a school was lacking in proofs for its opinions it straightway forged them, and was sure not to be found out. A vast mass of literature arose, which no man, with medieval implements, could detect, and effectually baffled and deceived the student of tradition. At every point he was confronted by imaginary canons and constitutions of the apostles, acts of Councils, decretals of early Popes, writings of the Fathers from St. Clement to St. Cyril, all of them composed for the purpose of deceiving.[135]

Writing in the same vein Lord Acton wrote:

> The passage from the Catholicism of the Fathers to that of the modern Popes was accomplished by willful falsehood; and the whole structure of traditions, laws and doctrines that support the theory of infallibility and the practical despotism of the Popes stands on a basis of fraud.[136]

The evidence of these extensive forgeries of course, begs the question; if there was absolute evidence of

---

135 Lecures on Modern History, page 78, Lord Acton, MacMillan & Co. Ltd., London, 1960.

136 North British Review, October 1869, page 130.

Rome's supreme universal jurisdiction, then why the necessity to forge?

CHAPTER VI

The Donation of Constantine

We now come to the most famous forgery of the middle ages found in the Pseudo-Isidorean Decretals, that of the Donation of Constantine supposedly written circa 320 and which *The Cambridge Medieval History* describes as the "cornerstone of papal power."[137] For over 600 years this document was an unqualified success in advancing papal claims. Documents so successful that its authenticity was unquestioned, even by the enemies of Rome.[138]

The Donation of Constantine professes to be a title deed or deed of gift from the Roman Emperor to Pope Sylvester in gratitude for the Pope having cured him of leprosy, "For when a horrible and filthy leprosy invaded all the flesh of my body.....the apostles SS. Peter and Paul appeared to me ..... Therefore I rose from sleep and followed the advice of the holy apostle..... The blessed Sylvester imposed on me a period of penance.....I rose from the water cleansed.....from the filthiness of leprosy." This grateful Emperor then conveys on the: ".....most blessed Sylvester, our father, supreme pontiff and universal pope of the city of

---

137 The Cambridge Medieval History, Vol. 11, page 586.

138 Byzantium, The Early Centuries, page 379, John Julius Norwich, Viking, The Penguin Group, London, 1988.

Rome,..... he shall have rule as well over the four principal sees, Antioch, Alexandria, Constantinople and Jerusalem, as also over all the churches of God in all the world." An egregious blunder by the forger because Constantinople and Jerusalem had not yet been elevated to patriarchal sees; in fact Jerusalem was not declared a see until the Council of Chalcedon in 451 - some 130 years later. Elsewhere Constantine was calling himself the conqueror of the Huns fifty years prior to their entering Europe. "..... and to the pontiffs, his successors, who to the end of the world shall sit in the seat of blessed Peter, we grant and by this present we convey our imperial Lateran palace, which is superior to and excels all palaces in the whole world.....". Constantine then hands over all the royal insignia of his imperial office: ".....the diadem, which is the crown of our head; and the mitre; as also the super-humeral, that is, the stole which usually surrounds our imperial neck; and the purple cloak and the scarlet tunic and all the imperial robes....."

This charming tale ends with the Emperor Constantine humbly informing Pope Sylvester that he is moving his government from Rome to Byzantium. ".....for it is not right that an earthly emperor should have authority there, where the rule of priests and the head of the Christian religion have been established by the Emperor of Heaven....." As a final act of fawning self- abasement the Emperor Constantine offers to act as Pope Sylvester's groom. To appreciate the irony of this, one only has to read the letters of the popes to the Roman Emperors, to see how very deferential they are.

Certainly not the kind of letters they would write to their grooms. The Donation of Constantine then, was a major attempt at revisionist history. "Parts of it were included in most of the medieval collections of canon law; Anslem's, Deusdedit's, and Gratian's great work (the Decretum, or Concordia discordantium canonum)",[139] in order to show the Christian world that Rome had always exercised supreme universal jurisdiction.

If you are ever in Rome you should visit the fortress-like monastery and church of SS. Quattro Coronati perched on the Coelian Hill. In the adjoining convent there is the little Oratory of Pope St. Sylvester built in the Byzantine tradition, where you will find a series of frescoes detailing the lives of the Emperor Constantine and Pope Sylvester; they date from 1246. One of these frescoes depicts the Donation of Constantine. Here the Emperor is standing and handing to a seated Pope St. Sylvester with his right hand, his crown symbolizing political power in Italy and the West, while in his left he holds as a groom, the reigns of the Pope's horse. From this famous forgery the reformed papacy adopted by right all the trappings of imperial majesty, a symbol of temporal power, reflected in Gregory's Dictus Papae No. 8 (That he alone may use the imperial insignia). St. Bernard of Clairvaux denounced this imperial papacy when he rebuked his formal pupil Bernard Paganelli (Pope Eugenius III, 1145 - 1153), "Peter is not known ever to have gone in procession adorned in jewels and

---

139 The Treatis of Loranenza Valla on the Treatise of the Donation of Constantine, page l, Text and translation by Christopher B. Coleman, University of Toronto Press. 1993.

silks, nor crowned with gold, nor mounted on a white horse, nor surrounded by knights, nor encircled by clamoring servants..... In these respects you are the heir not of Peter but of Constantine."[140] This imperial papacy endured for 900 years, until Pope John Paul I, breaking with tradition chose not to be installed by right of coronation. Refusing the visible symbols of temporal and monarchical authority, he was installed at a solemn mass substituting the tiara, for the palium, a white woolen stole symbolizing his pastoral role.

In his negotiations with Constantinople in 1054, Pope Leo IX resorted to "huge quotations from the Donation of Constantine",[141] as a prized "authority for his claims",[142] over the Eastern Church. Pope Gregory VII refers to the Donation of Constantine in the preceding oath to be given to kings; "As regards the regulation of churches and the lands or revenues given to St. Peter by the Emperor Constantine...." The first pope to make a territorial claim by explicitly referring to the Donation of Constantine was Pope Urban II in 1091 when he laid claim to Corsica. Urban also claimed the Italian Islands of Lipari for the papacy in the same year.[143]

The English Pope Adrian IV (Nicholas Breakspear) 1154-1159, bestowed Ireland to England's King Henry II, recognizing that it was his to dispose of, based on the

---

140 De Consideratione, IV. 3.6: (n.6) 776A. Bernard of Clairvaux.

141 Morris, page 137.

142 Papadadis, page 52.

143 The Papacy 1073 - 1198, page 310, I. S. Robinson, Cambridge University Press, 1993.

Donation of Constantine. As witnessed by the English historian John of Salisbury in 1159; 'At my request (Adrian IV) conceded and gave Ireland as a hereditary position to the illustrious king of the English, Henry II, as his letter still bears witness today. For all islands are said to belong to the Roman church by ancient right, according to the donation of Constantine, who richly endowed it.'[144] Adrian's immediate successor Pope Alexander III wrote a letter in September 1172 to King Henry II congratulating him on his victories in Ireland where he reminded Henry that the Donation of Constantine had given the papacy sovereignty over the island.[145] The great Italian poet Dante laments the Emperor Constantine's donation of temporal power to the papacy in a famous passage from his *Divine Comedy*;

> (Ah Constantine, how great an evil sprang
> Not from thine own conversion, but that gift
> That first rich Father did receive from thee!)
>
> *Inferno,* xix, 115 –17

[144] Ibid., page 310-311.
[145] Ibid., page 312.

CHAPTER VI

ROME CLINGS TO THE LEGEND AND ANNULS MAGNA CARTA

The sleuth who unmasked the Donation of Constantine as a forgery, was an Italian renaissance scholar named Lorenzo Valla (1407-1457). By using critical analysis of style and content Valla refuted some of the legal and historical claims and attacked the Donation of Constantine as a basis of temporal power of the papacy and urged Pope Eugenius to abandon the document as a fraud. His work brought him hostility and persecution and it was King Alfonso V of Aragon and Sicily who saved him from the Inquisition. His fortunes changed for the better when in 1448 the new Pope Nicholas V, the first of the Renaissance Popes, recognizing his extraordinary ability, made him apostolic secretary.

The Donation of Constantine with its impressive claims, had enormous influence in the formation of the Medieval Papacy and dominated the imagination of the Western Church. So much so, that nearly eighty years after being thoroughly discredited as a forgery, Pope Leo X commissioned Raphael to paint a huge mural dedicated to the myth in the *Sala di Constantino* in St. Peters. Even in the late nineteenth century, Rome could not let go of the legend. As we see it recorded in the *Roman Breviary* under *The Lesson for St. Sylvester's Day* (December 31) First Addition of 1879, Volume 1, page 250:

> Sylvester was a Roman by birth, and his father's name was Ruffinus. .....In his thirtieth year he was ordained Priest of the Holy Roman Church by Pope Marcellinus. In the discharge of his duties he became a model for all the clergy, and, after the death of Melchiades, he succeeded him on the Papal throne, in the year of Our Lord, 314. Constantine was then Emperor. This prince was afflicted with leprosy, and was advised by his physicians to bathe in children's blood, which he accordingly ordered to be shed for that purpose. The holy Apostles Peter and Paul appeared to him when he was asleep; and bade him, if he would be cleansed of his leprosy, abandon the atrocious thought of the bath; seek out Sylvester.....obeying his heavenly warning, caused Sylvester to be diligently sought for and brought before him. The Saint enabled him to recognize the Apostles by their images; healed him of his leprosy by baptism; and stirred him up to protect and propagate the religion of Christ. (Marquis of Bute's translation).

Even in the new version of 1908, Second Edition, page 172 col. (3), the legend lives on as a sort of apologetic memory:

> .....and there was an old story in the Church of Rome that it was Sylvester who caused him to recognize the images of the Apostles, administered to him holy Baptism, and cleansed him from the

leprosy of misbelief. (Marquis of Bute's translation).[146]

The temporal power of the papacy reached its height during the pontificate of Innocent III (1198-1216). Under this brilliant and energetic pope, "the kingdoms of Bulgaria, Portugal and England were made papal fiefs."[147] England became a papal fief as a result of an investiture controversy. The See of Canterbury became vacant and King John of England refused Pope Innocent's candidate, English Cardinal Stephen Langton. As a result Pope Innocent placed England under a papal interdict in 1208 and excommunicated King John in 1209. Under a papal interdict all sacraments were suspended, all business dealing were invalid, all trading was illegal and all Christians were forbidden contact.

By 1214 John was facing the prospect of invasion by the French King Philip anxious to exploit John's predicament. John capitulated; he accepted Stephen Langton and surrendered his kingdom to the papacy who returned it to him as a papal fief. King John also had to compensate the church 100,000 gold marks for its losses during the six years of interdiction, plus an annual payment of one thousand gold marks to the

---

146 As quoted in Papal Infallibility, page 271, 272, G. G. Coulton, Litt. D., D. Litt., LL.D., F.B.A. Fellow of St. John's and Hon. Fellow of St. Catharine's College, Cambridge. The Faith Press, London, 1932.

147 Encyclopaedia of Religion, Vol. II, page 177, MacMillan Publishing, New York, 1987.

papacy as a vassal[148] before Pope Innocent would lift the king's excommunication.[149] An interesting postscript to this story is that Stephen Langton, now Archbishop of Canterbury, led the restless English barons into demanding a solemn grant of liberties from King John which resulted in the Magna Carta, the first great charter of rights. King John signed this in 1215. That same year Pope Innocent excommunicated the rebel barons, suspended Stephen Langton and annulled Magna Carta.[150]

It should not be inferred that the popes, in using the Pseudo-Isidorean Decretals including the Donation of Constantine, were aware of their forged character. For the most part they were well-intentioned men who attempted to build a Christian Commonwealth under papal leadership, but this grand vision foundered when their temporal claims collided with the birth of the nation state. As the Italian poet Dante observed; "The Church of Rome commingling in herself two ruling powers, falls into the mud and soils herself and her task". *Divine Comedy, Purgatorio, Canto XVI.* The evils of papal temporal power, are revealed in the following lamentation:

---

148 Encyclopaedia Britannica, Vol. 13, page 25, William Benton, Publisher, 1972.

149 The Two Cities, Medieval Europe 1050 - 1320, Page 330, Malcolm Barber, Routledge, London & New York, 1994.

150 The Popes, A Concise Biographical History, Vol. 1, page 225, Edited by Eric John, MA., F.R.Hist.S., Hawthorn Books, Inc., New York, 1964.

CHAPTER VI

It is now more than a thousand years since these territories and cities have been given to the priests and ever since then the most violent wars have been waged on their account, and yet the priests neither now possess them in peace, nor will ever be able to possess them. It were in truth better before the eyes of God and the world that these pastors should entirely renounce the dominium temporale: for since Sylvester's time the consequences of the temporal power have been innumerable wars and the overthrow of peoples and cities. How is it possible that there has never been any good pope to remedy such evils and that so many wars have been waged for these transient possessions. Truly we cannot serve God and Mammon at the same time, cannot stand with one foot in Heaven and the other on earth.

Giovanni de'Mussi,
Chronicle of Piacenza, c. 1350

THE ORTHODOX RESPONSE TO ROMAN CLAIMS

One continually reads and hears in Roman Catholic circles that the schism between East and West was largely the fault of the Orthodox, i.e. it was their stubborn refusal to submit to the authority of the papacy that caused the cleavage. However, as we have seen, it is the Western Church under the Gregorian Reformers that must shoulder the lion's share of the blame. It was they who separated themselves from the 1,000 years of common collegial tradition which had bound both churches together.

The Roman Catholic historian Francis Dvornik, explains how the Orthodox were unaware of the immense changes taking place in the West under the reforming popes. To compound this, the forged Decretals of Pseudo-Isidore, which the reforming popes used to support their claims of authority, were incomprehensible to the Orthodox. In their efforts to raise the power and prestige of the papacy, the reformers went much further than some of their predecessors in claiming, not only supreme jurisdiction over the church and her bishops, but also "in their ignorance of the liturgical and ecclesiastical differences which existed in the churches in the East, complete conformity to Roman usage's in the East and in the West."[151] To the new found claims of temporal power with all its monarchical trappings, the Orthodox world could only gape in amazement.

The Orthodox response to this reformed papacy is best expressed by Nicetas, Archbishop of Nicomedia in the 12th century:

> My dearest brother, we do not deny to the Roman Church the primacy amongst the five sister Patriarchates; and we recognize her right to the most honourable seat at an Oecumenical Council. But she has separated herself from us by her own deeds when through pride she assumed a monarchy

[151] Byzantium and the Roman Primacy, page 166, Francis Dvornik, Fordham University Press, New York.

which does not belong to her office….. How shall we accept from her decrees that have been issued without consulting us and even without our knowledge? If the Roman Pontiff, seated on the lofty throne of his glory, wishes to thunder at us and, so to speak, hurl his mandates at us from on high, and if he wishes to judge us and even to rule us and our Churches, not by taking council with us but at his own arbitrary pleasure, what kind of brotherhood, or even what kind of parenthood can this be? We should be the slaves, not the sons, of such a Church, and the Roman See would not be the pious mother of sons but a hard and imperious mistress of slaves.[152]

---

152 The Eastern Schism, A Study of the Papacy and the Eastern Churches During the XIth and XIIth Centuries, Steven Runciman, Oxford at the Clarendon Press, 1956.

CHAPTER VII

Papal Infallibility

It was the morning of July 18th, 1870 and the heavy black clouds gathered and brooded over Rome, as the First Vatican Council convened for its final vote on the doctrine of Papal Infallibility. As the definition passed, a violent electrical storm broke out with the lightning lighting up the great hall above the Portico of St. Peter's where the assembled bishops were gathered. The storm smashed a window cascading shards of broken glass close to the pontifical throne.[153] When Pius IX had confirmed the declaration, the assembled bishops broke out with cheering and clapping. The Te Deum was then sung with the thunder of the storm offering a booming obligato. Opponents of the definition saw the storm as a sign of Divine anger; while its supporters reminded people that the Ten Commandments were given to Moses on Mount Sinai amidst the sound of thunder.

On the following day, war was declared between France and Prussia and on September 20th, Italian troops breached the walls of Rome and the Pope ordered the defending papal troops to surrender. The Papal States had breathed their last and the temporal power of the papacy was at an end with Pius IX as prisoner of the Vatican. The declaration of Papal Infallibility states in its final clause:

---

153 The Vatican Council, 1869 - 1870, page 416, Dom. Cuthbert Butler, Collins and Harvill Press, London, 1962.

> the Roman Pontiff, when he speaks *ex cathedra,* that is, when, as Shepherd and Teacher of all Christians, by virtue of his supreme apostolic authority he defines that a doctrine on faith or morals must be held by the Universal Church, enjoys, by the divine assistance promised to him in the person of Blessed Peter, that infallibility which the divine Redeemer intended His Church to possess when defining doctrine concerning faith and morals; and therefore, such definitions of the Roman Pontiff are unalterable in themselves and not by virtue of the assent of the Church.

This declaration erected a great formidable, some would say insurmountable barrier, to any future communion with the Orthodox Church, which views Papal Infallibility as an attempt to overthrow the collegial system of government that is intrinsic to the very nature of the church. We should examine the doctrine of Papal Infallibility in light of the ancient rule of the church, i.e. the dictum of St. Vincent of Lerins. Like many rules, it can be criticized when pushed to extremes; however, it has served as a magnificent rule of faith:

> In the Catholic Church care is especially to be taken that we hold that what has been believed everywhere, always, and by all: For this indeed is truly Catholic, as the very force and meaning of the word signifies, comprehending as it does in general all truth universally. And this will indeed be ours if we follow *Universality, Antiquity, and Consent.* We shall follow Universality if we confess that to

> be the one true faith which the whole Church throughout the world confesses; Antiquity also if we in no respect recede from those tenets which it is manifest that our holy Elders and Fathers held; and Consent, if in this antiquity we follow the definitions and opinions held by all or nearly all the ancient Bishops and Doctors.[154]

Councils of the Church can never define new dogma, they can only define dogmatic decrees on articles of faith that the Universal Church has always confessed. Thus Councils generally declared their acceptance of a dogmatic decree with the cry of, *Haec Fides Patrum,* (this is the Faith of the Fathers). Furthermore, the Church has historically been remarkably reticent in that she has defined dogma only when she absolutely had to, e.g. in the face of heretical opposition.

When we apply this ancient rule of faith, Papal Infallibility does not meet the criteria of *Universality, Antiquity and Consent.* The Scriptural passage most relied on to support Papal Infallibility is Luke XXII:32, "But I have prayed for thee, that thy faith fail not: and thou, being once converted, confirm the brethren.". Without exception none of the Church Fathers interpreted this passage as Christ conferring an infallible authority on St. Peter. American historian Brian Tierney on commenting on this text observes that: "There is no lack of patristic commentary on the text. None of the Fathers interpreted it as meaning that

154 Patrologiae Cursus Completus, S. Vincent Lirinensis, Commonitorium Primum adv. Haereses, c.ii., Migne.

Peter's successors were infallible. No convincing argument has ever been put forward explaining why they should not have stated that the text implied a doctrine of papal infallibility if that is what they understood it to mean."[155] Tierney points out that even in the early twelve hundreds, one of the great Decretists of the Church, Huguccio, did not look upon Luke 22:32 as conferring infallibility on the person of Peter:

> *That your faith shall not fail* is understood to mean finally and irrecoverably, for, although it failed for a time, afterwards he was made more faithful. Or in the person of Peter the church is understood, in the faith of Peter the faith of the universal church which has never failed as a whole nor shall fail down to the day of judgment. [156]

Another influential Decretist, Johannes Teutonicus saw the unfailing faith of the Church as promised by Christ in *Luke XXII:32,* surviving in Mary rather than Peter:

> *That your faith shall not fail,* that is the faith of the church which is your faith, for the church has never failed because it existed even at the Lords death at

---

155 Origins of Papal Infallibility 1150 - 1350, A Study on the Concepts on Infallibility, Sovereignty and Tradition in the Middle Ages. Page 11, Brian Tierney. From the series, Studies in the History of Christian Thought. E. J. Brill, Leiden, Netherlands, 1972.

156 Summa Ad Dist. 21, ante c. 1, MS Pembroke Coll. 72, fol. 129 vb. As quoted by Tierney.

> least in the Blessed Virgin. The church can be small; it cannot be nothing.[157]

French historian Yves Congar, made an exhaustive study of the concept of infallibility as the Church understood it in the middle ages and he concludes from the historical evidence that: "The basic conviction, universally shared, is that the Church herself cannot err (Albert the Great, Thomas Aquinas, Bonaventure, decretists). This is understood as the Church in her totality, as *congregatio* or universitas *fidelium.* One part or another of the Church can err, even the bishops, even the pope; the Church can be storm-tossed: in the end she remains faithful. In this sense Matthew 28:20 is quoted and even 16:18; Luke 22:32; John 16:13."

As we have seen in the preceding chapters, supreme universal jurisdiction resided in the general councils of the Church, not in the Bishop of Rome. One cannot see even a germ, or seminal seed for Papal Infallibility. Even if the Western Church could produce an argument for infallibility, the complete incomprehensibility of the Eastern Church to this doctrine would in itself crush the argument that Papal Infallibility was supported by the ancient maxim of *Universality, Antiquity and Consent.* It is provable beyond doubt that no teaching tradition of the church concerning Papal Infallibility presented itself to the canonists of the 12th and 13th centuries when they sifted through vast quantities of texts in order to create a

157 Summa Cantabrigiensis, MS Trinity College, Cambridge, 0.5.17, fol. 8 va, ad Dist. 21 ante c.1. As quoted by Tierney.

systematic code of canon law.[158] In spite of the lofty claims of pontiffs like Gregory the VII, medieval canonists such as Johannes Teutonicus, still reflected the traditional view of the church as to the supremacy of a general council:

> It seems that the pope is bound to require a council of bishops, which is true where a matter of faith is concerned, and then a council is greater than a pope, 15 dist. Sicut.[159]

The English canonist Alanus states:

> It is argued that in a matter of faith a council is greater than a pope.....and this is to be held firmly. It is for this reason that a council can judge and condemn him, and so it happens that he incurs the excommunication decreed for heresy in a council, which would not be the case if the pope was greater than the council in such a matter or equal to it.[160]

Alanus further writes:

> It is true that for the one crime of heresy a pope can be judged even against his own will. It is so in this crime because, in matters that pertain to the faith, he is less than the college of cardinals or a general council of bishops.[161]

---

158 Tierney, page 12.

159 Gl. Ord. ad Dist. 19 c.9, s.v. Concilio. .As quoted by Tierney.

160 Gloss ad Dist. 19 c. 9. As quoted by Tierney.

161 Gloss ad C. 9 q. 3 c. 17. As quoted by Tierney.

PAPAL INFALLIBILITY IS CREATED

Through his historical research Brian Tierney has shown that Papal Infallibility did not develop slowly, but was created by members of the Franciscan Order in the latter part of the 13th century because, "it suited their convenience to invent it", when Pope John XXII attacked their doctrine of evangelical poverty. In 1324, Pope John XXII condemned Papal Infallibility as a *pernicious novelty.*[162] This interesting pope's election came after two years of violent quarrels and bloodshed between rival factions. On June 28th, 1316 the exasperated French King Philip V, ordered his troops to surround the Dominican priory, in Lyons, where the cardinals were in session and told them that they were considered prisoners until they elected a pope. To extricate themselves from this desperate situation, a compromise candidate was elected in the person of Cardinal Jacques Duese, Bishop of Porto.

The son of a shoemaker, John was a dry, wisp-like little man who as a lawyer had assisted in gathering and arranging evidence against the Knights Templars. He was also a keen accountant and was known as the *Banker of Avignon* - his meticulous ledgers are still preserved in the Vatican. Now a frail old man of 72, looking more like the *ghost of Christmas past,* he was ushered out of the conclave as Pope John XXII by the anxious cardinals as their price of freedom. However, to the astonishment and perhaps dismay of his electors, the papal office seems to have given this cranky, bad

---

[162] Tierney, page 188.

tempered, iron willed prelate, a new lease on life - for he lived another 18 years, displaying an astonishing vigour as a gifted administrator. He even survived two attempts on his life early in his pontificate – one by poisoning and another by witchcraft.

Pope John XXII's problem was that infallibility carried with it the necessity of irreformability, i.e. popes are limited in their ability to revoke the decrees of their successors. Irreformability was at the centre of his bitter conflict with the leaders of the Franciscans when he revoked Pope Nicholas III's Bull *Exiit*, promulgated in August 1279. This Bull was enthusiastically received by the Franciscan Order because, "Pope Nicholas III not only approved the Franciscan way of life as his predecessors had done", but, "For the first time he affirmed as an official teaching of the Roman Church the Franciscans assertion that their way of life was the very way of perfection that Christ had revealed to the Apostles".[163] Historian Brian Tierney explains Pope John's dilemma:

> The Franciscans taught that the perfect way of life which Christ had shown to Peter and the apostles required the abdication of all dominion, all usufruct, all right of use. If this were true then pope and bishops had long ago abandoned the ideal of Peter and the apostles. It was not simply that individual prelates failed to live up to the ideal. Rather, the ordered, visible structure of the hierarchical church failed to exemplify the Christian ideal at all. If the

[163] Ibid., page 97 - 98.

> Franciscans were right about the essence of the evangelical life then John XXII and his bishops were not "successors" of Peter and the apostles in any full and meaningful sense of the word. And yet the Franciscan doctrine seemed to be supported by the plain words of the decretal *Exiit.* John XXII evidently came to the conclusion that his predecessor, Nicholas III, had made radical blunders in his dealings with the Franciscans – blunders concerning both church discipline and church doctrine. John was determined to use his sovereign authority as head of the church to correct those blunders.[164]

The Franciscan leaders defended this cherished papal Bull on the grounds that it was irreformable and its very "irreformability" logically presupposed Papal Infallibility. John XXII was not interested in his own infallibility anymore than his predecessors. For him infallibility would place him, as it would his successors, in a straight jacket, i.e. limiting the powers of the reigning pope by the infallible declarations of their predecessors. In March of 1322, Pope John XXII issued a Bull *Extravagantes,* in which he maintains a reigning pope's right to annul the judgments and decrees of his predecessors:

> Because sometimes what conjecture believed would prove profitable subsequent experience shows to be harmful, it ought not to be thought reprehensible if

164 Ibid., page 175.

> the founder of the canons decides to revoke, modify or suspend the canons put forth by himself or his predecessors.[165]

He issued another Bull *Quia Quorundam* in November 1324, in which he contemptuously proclaims irreformability as a "pernicious audacity" and that the "Father of lies", have led his opponents to declare:

> What the Roman pontiffs have once defined in faith and morals with the key of knowledge stands so immutably that it is not permitted to a successor to revoke it.[166]

The fascinating aspect of this whole controversy is the emergency of the doctrine of Papal Infallibility and its angry denouncement by the reigning pontiff. It is only in the 16th century that we find a serious revival of Papal Infallibility among Catholic theologians.[167]

Many Catholic historians and apologists admit, that there is scant evidence for Papal Infallibility in the historical record and so attempt to overcome the difficulty, by suggesting that while popes possessed the gift of infallibility, they were not aware of it. *Radio Replies,* a popular work of Catholic apologetics puts the argument this way:

---

165 Extravagantes D. Ioannis XXII in E. Friedberg (ed.), Corpus Iuris Canonici, II (Leipzig, 1879), Tit. 14 c. 2, col. 1224. As quoted by Tierney.

166 Tierney, page 186.

167 Ibid., page 271.

Before the definition of infallibility in 1870, the Popes did not know that they were infallible with the same full certainty of faith as that possessed by later Popes. They were infallible in fact.[168]

THE GREAT SCHISM AND THE COUNCIL OF CONSTANCE

The Great Schism that lasted 40 years witnessed the sad spectacle of three popes, hurling excommunications and anathemas at each other and dividing the loyalties of Europe. At one point, Pope Alexander V commanded the allegiance of a large part of Western Europe - Pope Gregory XII held the allegiance of Naples and some of the Italian states, while Pope Benedict XIII had Spain and Scotland on his side. Something had to be done - but what? How could a general council dispose of a canonically elected pope, when only a pope had the authority to call a council. Conrad of Gelnhausen, provost of Worms, dryly explains this rather silly legal bind:

> It is impossible for the general council to be held or celebrated without the authority of the pope. But to convene such a council in the present case the authority of the pope cannot step in, because no single person is universally recognized as pope, nor is any individual generally obeyed as pope, and if

168 Radio Replies, page 96, Vol. 3, Fathers Rumble and Carty, Tan Books and Publishers Inc., Rockford, Illinois. 1979.

> the council were to be convoked by the authority of the one or the other person now in question, he would in virtue of this be recognized as pope; and from this it is to be inferred that they cannot both authorize it, because there cannot be more than one supreme pontiff.[169]

It was obvious that all three popes had to go in order to end this deplorable situation. Since one of these men was the real pontiff, it was necessary that a council be convened that would be recognized by the entire church, as having a higher authority than a pope. Ultimately, the German Emperor convened a general council at Constance in 1414, however; "for many contemporaries, a council possessing sovereign power superior to the pope, was seen as a positively freakish way to resolve the schism".[170]

The Council of Constance was convened on November 5th, 1414 and it was one of the greatest councils held in the West. In attendance were three patriarchs, twenty-nine cardinals, thirty-three archbishops, one hundred and fifty bishops, one hundred abbots, three hundred doctors of theology, eighteen hundred priests and over one hundred dukes, earls and twenty- four hundred knights. One archbishop brought six hundred horses with him, which in winter placed a

---

169 Epistola Concordiae, F. Blienetzrieder, ed., Literarische Polemik zu Beginn des grossen Abendlandischen Schismas (Vienna, 1910), 127. As quoted by Tierney.

170 The Christian East and the Rise of the Papacy, page 371, Aristeides Papadakas in collaboration with John Meyendorff, St Vladimir's Seminary Press, Crestwood, New York, 1994.

great strain on the hay supply, a regulation was therefore passed which restricted Pope John XXIII to twenty horses, the cardinals to ten each, the bishops to five and the abbots to four. The Council recognized Pope John XXIII as the legitimate pope and he authorized its gathering. This great council declared in true patristic tradition that it is a general council of the Church that holds supreme universal jurisdiction, not the pope:

> This sacred synod of Constance.....declares.....that it has its power immediately from Christ, and that all men, of every rank and position, including the pope himself, are bound to obey it in those matters that pertain to the faith, the extirpation of the said schism, and to the reformation of the Church in head and members. It declares also that anyone, of any rank, condition or office - even the papal - who shall contumaciously refuse to obey the mandates, statutes, decrees or instructions made by this holy synod or by any other lawfully assembled council on the matters aforesaid or on things pertaining to them, shall, unless he recovers his senses, be subjected to fitting penance and punished as is appropriate.[171]

This council ended the Great Schism by deposing two popes and compelling John XXIII, whom they recognized as the legitimate pope, to resign due to his scandalous life. The pope yielded to the sentence, thus

171 Sacrorum Conciliorum Nova et Amplissima Collectio, 27:590, J. D. Mansi, Florence, 1759 - 63.

recognizing that he was subject to the supreme authority of the council. The council elected Pope Martin V who solemnly swore that he would uphold all the decrees of the Council of Constance, thus explicitly recognizing its authority. He then issued a Bull *Inter Cunctas* in which a test of faith is given by the following questions: "Do you believe, hold and maintain that every General Council, and especially that of Constance, represents the universal Church? Do you believe that all the faithful are obliged to approve and believe what the holy Council of Constance representing the universal Church has approved and approves touching the faith and the salvation of souls, and what it condemned and condemns as contrary to the faith and good morals?"[172] As Bishop Maret, Dean of the University of Paris, observed, "Can there be anything more formal, more decisive than these words in favour of the indivisible authority of the Council of Constance."[173]

PREVIOUS INFALLIBLE DECLARATIONS CONTRADICTED

The critics of papal infallibility warned the Church that if this was passed as dogma, then all the embarrassing decrees of previous councils and papal bulls dealing with usury, (earning interest on loans), the denial of religious liberty, salvation etc., would come

172 Compendium of Ecclesiastical History, vol. IV, page 307. Johann C.L. Gieseler.

173 Du Concile General et de Paix Religieuse, Vol.i, page 399. Bishop Maret.

back to haunt it with a vengeance. The truth of this prophecy maybe judged by the following contradictory declarations. The first of which dealing with religious liberty, was issued to the entire Church with all due solemnity in 1215 by the Fourth Lateran Council:

> We excommunicate and anathematize every heresy that raises itself against the holy, orthodox and Catholic faith.....Secular authorities, whatever office they may hold shall be admonished and induced and if necessary compelled by ecclesiastical censure, that as they wish to be esteemed and numbered among the faithful, so for the defense of the faith they ought publicly to take an oath that they will strive in good faith and to the best of their ability to exterminate in the territories subject to their jurisdiction all heretics pointed out by the church.[174]

In 1965 the Second Vatican Council declared however, that:

> This Vatican Synod declares that the human person has a right to religious freedom. This freedom means that all men are to be immune from coercion.....in such wise that in matters religious no one is to be forced to act in a manner contrary to his

174 The Disciplinary Decrees of the General Councils, page 242, H.J. Schroeder, St. Louis, 1937.

own beliefs. Nor is anyone to be restrained from acting in accordance with his own beliefs.[175]

Some may argue that the declaration of the Fourth Lateran Council is not an infallible statement. However, the following papal bulls of Boniface VIII and Eugene IV, confirming that there is no salvation outside the Catholic Church is clothed in the language of ex cathedra declarations[176] e.g., "We declare, define.....firmly believe, profess, and preach....." The following popes made these declarations to all the faithful from the chair (ex cathedra) as the supreme head of the Church. A more explicit exercise of papal infallibility would be difficult to find as the following well illustrates:

> Indeed we declare, say, pronounce, and define that it is altogether necessary to salvation for every human creature to be subject to the Roman Pontiff. Pope Boniface VIII, Papal Bull *Unam Sanctam,* 1302.

> The most Holy Roman Catholic Church firmly believes, professes, and preaches that none of those existing outside the Catholic Church, not only

---

175 The Documents of Vatican II, page 678, W.M. Abbott, New York, 1966.

176 The Catholic Catechism, page 235, John A. Hardon, S.J., Doubleday & Co., Garden City, New York, 1975. "Since the Fourth Lateran Council in 1215 defined that 'The universal Church of the faithful is one, outside of which no one is saved', there have two solemn definitions of the same doctrine, by Pope Boniface VIII in 1302 and at the Council of Florence in 1442".

> pagans, but also Jews and heretics and schismatics, can have a share in eternal life; but that they will go into the eternal fire which was prepared for the devil and his angels, unless before death they are joined with Her; and that so important is the unity of this ecclesiastical body that only those remaining within this unity can receive an eternal recompense for their fasts, their almsgivings, their other works of Christian piety and the duties of a Christian soldier. No one, let his almsgiving be as great as it may, no one, even if he pour out his blood for the name of Christ, can be saved, unless he remain within the bosom and the unity of the Catholic Church. Pope Eugene IV, Council of Florence, 1438-1445, from the Papal Bull *Cantate Domino,* 1441.

In keeping with this teaching, the Second Vatican Council states: "This sacred Synod turns its attention first to the Catholic faithful. Basing itself upon sacred Scripture and tradition, it teaches that the Church, now sojourning on earth as an exile, is necessary for salvation."[177] The Council then attempts to drain all meaning out of the previous declarations of Popes Boniface VIII and Eugene IV, by stating that salvation is only denied to those, "Whosoever, therefore, knowing that the Catholic Church was made necessary by God through Jesus Christ, would refuse to enter her or to remain in her could not be saved."

---

[177] The Documents of Vatican II, page 32, Walter M. Abbott, S.J. General Editor, Guild Press , New York, 1966.

This of course is an attempt to put a good spin on embarrassing infallible declarations, for the language of these papal bulls is perfectly clear – there is no salvation outside the Church. No qualifying statements were made that this only applies to those who knowingly deny the Catholic Church as the true Church. Pope Eugene even supplies the more obtuse with some examples, "No one let his almsgiving be as great as it may, no one, even if he pour out his blood for the name of Christ, can be saved, unless he remain within the bosom and unity of the Catholic Church."

Obviously someone with the courage and integrity to lay down his life for Christ would certainly not hesitate to embrace the Catholic Church if he thought it to be the true Church. Nevertheless, ignorance is no defense – salvation is denied. Besides, the teaching of St. Augustine that unbaptised infants are denied salvation, is in fact the teaching of the Western Church.[178] Limbo, (Limbus Infantum or Puerum) is in Roman Catholic theology the place where infants are consigned who died without actual sin (personal sin) – but who did not have their original sin washed away by baptism. The word Limbus or Limbo first appeared in the *Summa Theologica* of St. Thomas Aquinas. In this Limbo they are, ".....excluded from the full blessedness of the beatific vision....."[179] This teaching was declared *de fide,* by the Second Council of Lyons (1274) and

---

178 On Forgiveness of Sins, and Baptism, Chap. 21 (XVI.) St. Augustine.

179 Pocket Catholic Dictionary, page 228, John A. Hardon, S.J. Image Books, 1985.

confirmed by the Council of Florence (1439). Therefore, "it is an article of the Catholic faith that those who die without baptism, and for whom the want of baptism has not been supplied in some other way, cannot enter heaven. This is the teaching of the ecumenical councils of Florence and Trent."[180]

If it is an article of faith, that unbaptised infants who have committed no actual sin cannot merit salvation, what are the chances for Jews, pagans, heretics and schismatics? Again, the intent of the papal bulls are crystal clear in spite of the best efforts of the Second Vatican Council. This teaching was strenuously reiterated by more recent popes such as Pius IX who in his *Syllabus of Errors* condemned the following propositions:

15. Every man is free to embrace and profess that religion which, guided by the light of reason, he shall consider true. - - Allocution "Maxima quidem," June 9, 1862; Damnatio "Multiplices inter," June 10, 1851.

16. Man may, in the observance of any religion whatever, find the way of eternal salvation. - - Encyclical "Qui pluibus," Nov. 9, 1846.

17. Good hope at least is to be entertained of the eternal salvation of all those who are not at all in the true Church of Christ. - - Encyclical "Quanto conficiamur," Aug. 10, 1863, etc.

---

180 Ibid., page 229.

CHAPTER VII

To the Christians of other denominations, the Second Vatican Council now however, assures them that:

> The brethren divided from us also carry out many of the sacred actions of the Christian religion. Undoubtedly, in ways that vary according to the condition of each Church or Community, these actions can truly engender a life of grace, and can be rightly described as capable of providing access to the community of salvation.[181]

Salvation is available to non -Christians:

> But the plan of salvation also includes those who acknowledge the Creator. In the first place among these there are the Moslems, who, professing to hold the faith of Abraham, along with us adore the one and merciful God, who on the last day will judge mankind. [182]

Even to the pagans worshiping idols:

> Nor is God Himself far distant from those who in shadows and images seek the unknown God, for it is He who gives to all men life and breath and every other gift (cf. Acts 17:25-28), and who as Savior wills that all men be saved (cf. 1 Tim. 2:4).[183]

---

181 Ibid., page 346.

182 Ibid., page 35.

183 Ibid., page 35.

Last but not least, are the atheists for:

> Those also can attain to everlasting salvation who through no fault of their own do not know the gospel of Christ or His Church, yet sincerely seek God and, moved by grace, strive by their deeds to do His will as it is known to them through the dictates of conscience. Nor does divine Providence deny the help necessary for salvation to those who, without blame on their part, have not yet arrived at an explicit knowledge of God, but who strive to live a good life, thanks to His grace.[184]

Is there a more a glaring example of previous infallible declarations so sweepingly contradicted? The English Jesuit George Tyrrell's observation is very apt, "All infallible decrees are certainly true but no decrees are certainly infallible".

---

[184] Ibid., page 35.

CHAPTER VIII

Papal Infallibility Becomes Dogma

On September 8th, 1713, Pope Clement XI issued a Bull, *Unigenitus*, which among other things condemned the proposition that, "reading of the bible is for everyone",[185] and seemed to exalt the efficacy of grace to the point of destroying liberty. It also appeared to, "limit the Church to the predestined only."[186] The storm of protest that arose against it, proves conclusively that 18th century Catholic Europe had little notion of Papal Infallibility. This Papal Bull almost brought France to the brink of schism[187] and "the Austrian Emperor forbade the Bull *Unigenitus* in his territories".[188] This Bull sparked a debate as to the limits of papal authority. Sicilian seminaries were teaching their students that, "General Councils were supreme over the Pope" and were using *Unigenitus* "to show how Popes could err".[189] "Everywhere the battle over *Unigenitus*, caused a decline in the reputation of the See of Rome as a teacher of doctrinal truth."[190]

---

185 The Popes and European Revolution, page 75, Owen Chadwick, Clarendon Press, Oxford, 1981.

186 New Catholic Encyclopedia, page 397, Vol. XIV.

187 Ibid., page 398, Vol. VII.

188 Chadwick, page 238.

189 Chadwich, page 284.

190 Chadwick, page 285.

CHAPTER VIII

In 1789 the *Protestation of the English Catholics* was signed by all the vicars-general and 'all the Catholic clergy and laity in England of any note' and solemnly declared before Parliament, that 'we acknowledge no infallibility in the pope'[191] and even in 19th century England and Ireland, Papal Infallibility was still denied as an article of Catholic belief. In 1822 Bishop Baines Vicar Apostolic in England, wrote that 'Bellarmine, and some other divines, chiefly Italians, have believed the Pope infallible, when proposing *ex cathedra* an article of faith. But in England or Ireland I do not believe that any Catholic maintains the infallibility of the Pope'.[192] In 1825, a British Parliamentary Royal Commission was established in view of the forthcoming Catholic Emancipation Act of 1829. Some of the questions put to Roman Catholic Bishops are as follows:

Question to Bishop Doyle

Q: Is the authority of the Pope in spiritual matters absolute or limited?

A: It is limited.

Questions to Bishop Murray

Q: Is that (Papal) authority under the control of General Councils?

---

191 Historical Memoirs Respecting the English Catholics, ii, pages 113 - 118, Charles Butler, 1819.

192 A Defence of the Christian Religion, page 230, Bath, 1822. See W.E. Gladstone, Vaticanism page 48, 1875.

A: That authority is limited by the councils and canons of the Church; he is the executive power of the Church, appointed to preside over it, and enforce its canons or laws. Those canons vest in individuals, for instance in Bishops, certain rights, which of course is the duty of the Pope to protect, and not violate; his authority is thus limited by those canons.

Q: Does it justify an objection that is made to Catholics, that their allegiance is divided?

A: Their allegiance in civil matters is completely undivided.

Question to Dr. Oliver Kelley:

Q: Do the R.C. clergy insist that all the Bulls of the Pope are entitled to obedience?

A: The Roman Catholic doctrine in respect to Bulls from the Pope is that they are always to be treated with respect; but if those Bulls or Rescripts proceeding from the Pope do contain doctrines or matters which are not compatible with the discipline of the particular Church to which they may be directed, they feel it their duty then to remonstrate respectfully, and not to receive the regulations that may emanate from the Pope.

CHAPTER VIII

Question to Bishop Doyle:

Q: Can you state in what respect the national canons received in Ireland, or any particular construction put upon the general canons, differ from those which are received in other countries?

A: For instance, a particular church, or the canons of a particular church, might define that the authority of a general council was superior to that of the Pope: Such canon may be received, for instance in Ireland or France, and might not be received in Italy or Spain.

Question to Bishop Murray:

Q: Is the decree of the Pope valid without the consent of the Council?

A: A decree of the Pope in matters of doctrine is not considered binding on Catholics, if it have not the consent of the whole Church, either dispersed or assembled by its Bishops in Council.[193]

In 1826, the 'declaration of the Archbishops and Bishops of the Roman Catholic Church in Ireland', was endorsed by the signatures of 30 bishops, declaring that 'The Catholics of Ireland declare on oath their belief that it is not an article of the Catholic faith, neither are

---

193 Friedrich's Documenta, Vol. I, pages 234, 236, 237, 240.

they required to believe, that the pope is infallible'.[194] Archbishop Kenrick of St. Louis, pointed out in his undelivered speech, which he had published in Naples, that for two hundred years a book had been in circulation entitled, *Roman Catholic Principles in Reference to God and the King.* It enjoyed such a wide circulation that from 1748 to 1813 it underwent 35 editions and the Very Reverend Vicar Apostolic Coppinger in England had 12 printings of it. On the question of Papal Infallibility it states:

> It is no matter of faith to believe that the Pope is in himself infallible, separated from the Church, even in expounding the faith: by consequence of Papal definitions or decrees, in whatever form pronounced, taken exclusively from a General Council, or universal acceptance of the Church, oblige none, under pain of heresy, to an interior assent.[195]

PAPAL INFALLIBILITY - A PROTESTANT HOAX?

One of the most popular catechisms circulating in 19th century England was the *Controversial Catechism* by the Reverend Stephen Keenan. The one I have is the

194 Essay on the Catholic Claims, page 300, Bishop J.W. Doyle, 1826.
195 Kenrick (Naples edition). Page 46.

third edition of 1854, published by Marsh and Beattie of Edinburgh and Charles Dolman of London and Manchester. On page 112 we find the following question and answer:

> Q: Must not Catholics believe the Pope in himself to be infallible?
>
> A: This is a Protestant invention; it is no article of the Catholic faith; no decision of his can oblige, under pain of heresy, unless it be received and enforced by the teaching body; that is, by the bishops of the Church.

This catechism carries the enthusiastic approbation of four bishops:

BY THE RIGHT REV. BISHOP CARRUTHERS.

A concise summary of arguments, authorities, and proofs, in support of the doctrines, institutions and practices of the Catholic Church, is here presented in a very convenient form, as an additional antidote against the unceasing effusions of antagonistic Ignorance and Misrepresentation. .....The work I trust will meet with the notice it deserves, and the good be thus effected which the zealous and talented author has had in view of its publication.

ANDREW, BISHOP OF CERAMIS,

Vicar Apostolic of Eastern Scotland.

Edinburgh, 10th April, 1846.

BY THE RIGHT REV. BISHOP GILLIS.

I have much pleasure in adding my name to the above Approbation by my Venerable Predecessor, and in earnestly recommending the study of the CONTROVERSIAL CATECHISM to the Faithful of the Eastern District of Scotland. .....But there are many, it is to be hoped, sincere in their pursuit of Truth; and to all such, the CONTROVERSIAL CATECHISM must ever prove a welcome and highly useful guide.

The fact that nine thousand copies having already been exhausted in two Editions in this country, besides a third Edition printed in America, is evidence sufficient of the favour with which the Catechism has been received by the Catholic Public. .....

JAMES, BISHOP OF LIMYRA,

Vicar Apostolic of the Eastern District in Scotland.

Edinburgh, 14th November, 1853.

BY THE RIGHT REV. BISHOP KYLE.

I have read, with much pleasure, a Work entitled "Controversial Catechism, by the Rev. Stephen Keenan." As it contains a well reasoned defense of the Catholic faith, and clear and satisfactory solutions of the usual objections adduced by separatists, I deem that the study of it will be most useful to all Catholics; and, therefore, I earnestly recommend it to the Faithful in the Northern District of Scotland.

JAS. KYLE, V.A. N.D.S.

Preshome, 15th April, 1846.

BY THE RIGHT REV. BISHOP MURDOCH.

Glasgow, 19th November, 1853.

My Dear Mr. Keenan,

I am exceedingly delighted to learn that a Third Edition of your excellent "CONTROVERSIAL CATECHISM" is about to be printed. You request my approbation of this New Edition. Most willingly and most heartily do I give it. But it is really altogether unnecessary; for the work has amply approved itself. The rapid exhaustion of the last two editions, is more than sufficient proof of the value and worth of the Catechism. I know not, indeed, if we possess a better volume adapted to the wants of the time;.....As long as the CONTROVERSIAL CATECHISM is to be had, it is entirely the fault of all Catholics - be their rank however humble - if they be not ready on all occasions to give a reason of the faith and hope that are in them. I am, Rev. Dear Sir, yours sincerely in Christ,

JOHN MURDOCH, V.A. W.D.

The Rev. Stephen Keenan, Dundee.

PREFACE TO THE SECOND EDITION.

The rapid sale of the former edition, - its approbation by many Clergyman in Scotland and by several in Ireland and England, - the fact of its appearing in a very elegant American edition, approved by the Right Rev. Dr. Hughes of New York, and by the American Catholic Clergy and Catholic press, - combined with the antipathy of modern religionists to its publication or circulation, and the unwilling testimony wrung from them as to its efficacy in supporting truth, - all these motives, strengthened by a desire to put down error and establish truth, have induced the Author to give the public a second edition. .....

Thus here in mid-nineteenth century Britain and America, we have a very popular Catholic Catechism claiming the notion of Papal Infallibility as evidence of Protestant deceit or ignorance. As we have seen, this was not an article of faith that the universal church has always confessed. Pius IX had already tested infallibility, when in 1854 he declared the doctrine of the Immaculate Conception of, "which some of them (bishops) dreaded and some opposed, but which all submitted when he had decreed without the intervention of a Council."[196]

---

196 Essays on Freedom and Power, page 305, Lord Acton, Meridian Book, Cleveland, Ohio. 1972.

CHAPTER VIII

POPE PIUS IX - THE INFALLIBLE INSTRUMENT OF GOD

Count Giovanni Maria Mastai-Ferretti, the future Pius IX was born in 1792, being the last of nine children, to a family of the lesser nobility. In his youth and well into his thirties he suffered epileptic seizures. For a while he was allowed to celebrate mass only on the condition that another priest or deacon was present. Nothing more is heard of this condition in his later life, however according to his contemporaries the traces of the Pope's epilepsy were visible, in that the right side of his body was slightly less developed than the left. "This could be seen even in his face which was asymmetric, with lips awry and a head that inclined to the right."

Pius IX was the longest reigning pope, possessing personal charm and enjoying great popularity, he was also considered highly impressionable, capricious, impulsive and unpredictable. These characteristics were attributed to his epilepsy.[197] It is this Pope Pius IX who was absolutely determined to have his office dogmatically defined as the infallible instrument of God by a council of the Church.

At the First Vatican Council the approval of the passing of Papal Infallibility was almost guaranteed from the beginning. First, by the incredibly unequal representation which was highlighted during the

---

197 How the Pope Became Infallible, Pius IX and the Politics of Persuasion, page 107, August Bernhard Hasler, Translated by Peter Heinegg, Doubleday and Co. Inc., Garden City, New York, 1981.

Council by a pamphlet, whose author was believed to be Georges Darboy, Archbishop of Paris entitled, *The Liberty of the Council and the Infallibility.* This pamphlet claimed that while Italy had two hundred and seventy bishops, the rest of Europe had only two hundred and sixty-five. Closer scrutiny reveals that twelve million German Roman Catholics were represented by nineteen bishops while seven hundred thousand inhabitants of the Papal States were represented by sixty-two. Three anti-Infallibilist Bishops of Cologne, Paris and Cambrai represented five million souls. It is little wonder that the German bishops who formed the backbone of the anti-Infallibilist complained of being overwhelmed by Italian and Sicilian bishops.[198]

The second reason why the doctrine of Papal Infallibility was guaranteed to pass, was the deep personal involvement of Pius IX himself and the intimidating coercive tactics he used. A measure of his resolve is the statement he made to the chief editor of *La Civilta Cattolica,* "My mind is so made up that if need be I shall take the definition upon myself and dismiss the Council if it wishes to keep silence."[199] In a brief to Dom Gueranger, Abbot of Solesmes, a leading French Ultramontane (on the other side of the Alps; one who advocates supreme papal authority), Pius IX, while demonstrating no lack of confidence in his own infallibility, attacks and brands the bishops who oppose the definition as men, "who show themselves

198 Butler, The Vatican Council, page 230.

199 Hasler, page 81.

completely imbued with corrupt principals and who no longer know how to submit their intelligence to the judgment of the Holy See.....Their folly mounts to this excess that they attempt to remake the divine constitution of the Church in order to bring down more easily the authority of the supreme Head whom Christ has set over it and whose prerogatives they dread."[200] Pope Pius IX was so bent on having the office of the Papacy declared Infallible he used the power and prestige of his office to intimidate and upbraid even bishops who adopted a neutral or moderate line. The Reverend T. Mozley, special correspondent to The Times of London writes that bishops who adopted a neutral or moderate line:

> find themselves sorely tried in a personal interview. They find it vain to declare their devotion or their sincerity. His Holiness tells them plainly they are not on his side; they are among his enemies; they are damaging the good cause; their loyalty is not sound. It is enough that they have signed what they should not, or not signed what they ought.[201]

Ullathorne, Bishop of Birmingham wrote; "The Pope, takes every opportunity of expressing his views on the infallibility both in audiences and letters that at once get into the papers."[202] Again Ullathorne writes, "The Pope, I believe, is bent on the definition, if he can,

---

200 Friedrich, Documenta, Vol. i, page 184.
201 Letters from Rome, 11, 282.
202 Butler, The Vatican Council, Vol. ii, page 199.

as the crowning of his reign, and I think it will in some shape probably pass."[203] To a group of vicars apostolic and Oriental bishops, Pius IX reminded them, "It is necessary for you to defend the truth with the Vicar of Jesus Christ. My children do not abandon me."[204]

A stark example of how far removed the bishops, the successors of the apostles, were from the dignity and freedom they exercised at the Seven Ecumenical Councils and their subservience to the Pope can be judged by the behaviour of Wilhelm von Ketteler, Bishop of Mainz. Just before the final vote on Papal Infallibility, a deputation of minority bishops implored Pius IX to accept certain concessions in the wording of the declaration: Ketteler threw himself on his knees and with tears in his eyes said: 'Good Father, save us and save the Church of God!'[205] One cannot help recalling St. Paul's reproof to St. Peter when he, "withstood him to his face", Gal. 11:11, and St. Irenaeus' "stern rebuke" to Pope St. Victor over the Easter controversy, (see Chapter II). Pius was unmoved.

Cardinal Guidi, Archbishop of Bologna, in a speech before the Council said that, while accepting infallibility he urged the Pope to take the counsel of his bishops before issuing decisions as this is the tradition of the Church. Guidi's speech was reported to the Pope and he was sent for and scolded. The surprised Cardinal responded that he was only maintaining that bishops are witnesses of tradition, 'Witnesses of tradition?' said the

---

203 Ibid., page 119.
204 Friedrich, Documenta, Vol. i, page 185.
205 Butler, page 407.

Pope, 'There is only one; that's me.'[206] Even Roman Catholic author Dom. Cuthbert Butler in his popular work, *The Vatican Council*, admits to the personal influence of Pius IX, ... "did it amount to undue influence? That at the final stages he exerted his personal influence to the utmost cannot be questioned, for it was quite open."[207]

A COUNCIL LACKING IN FREEDOM

Strenuous objections were voiced at the Council, regarding the lack of freedom due to the manner of the agenda. Dom Butler admits to the Pope's control over the Council when he writes: "In all things the Pope kept to himself the complete mastery. Things which at Trent had been left in the hands of the Fathers - settlement of claims to take part in the Council, appointment of officials, regulation of procedure, etc. - were all now fixed by the personal act of the Pope.....The bishops were invited and exhorted to suggest freely anything for deliberation that they thought would be for the general good of the Church. But such proposals or postulations must be submitted to a special Congregation, nominated by the Pope, for dealing with such postulates, to consider them and report its advice to the Pope, with whom the decision would lie as to whether the thing be brought forward at the Council or not."[208]

---

[206] Ibid., page 355.
[207] Ibid., page 446.
[208] Ibid., page 213, 214.

Denying the validity of the Council, Archbishop Peter Richard Kenrick, 'refused to speak at any of the general sessions after June 4th, 1870. Bishop Joseph Strossmeyer of Diakovar told Lord Acton, 'There is no denying that the Council lacked freedom from beginning to end'. To Professor Joseph Hubert Reinkens, Strossmeyer said, "that the Vatican Council had not had the freedom necessary to make it a true Council and to justify its passing resolutions binding the conscience of the entire Catholic world. The proof of this was perfectly self-evident."[209]

Bishop Francois Le Courtier spoke for many when he wrote: 'Our weakness at this moment comes neither from scripture nor the tradition of the Fathers nor the witness of the General Councils nor the evidence of history. It comes from our lack of freedom, which is radical. An imposing minority, representing the faith of more than one hundred million Catholics, that is, almost half of the entire Church, is crushed beneath the yoke of a restrictive agenda, which contradicts conciliar traditions. It is crushed by commissions which have not been truly elected and which dare to insert undebated paragraphs in the text after debate has closed. It is crushed by the commission for postulates, which has been imposed from above. It is crushed by the absolute absence of discussion, response, objections, and the opportunity to demand explanations; .....The minority is crushed, above all, by the full weight of the supreme authority which oppresses it....'.[210] Furthermore, "the

---

209 Hasler, page 133.

210 Hasler, pages 131, 132.

opposing minority of about two hundred bishops objected to the short time allowed for studying the text on primacy and infallibility as well as to the practice adopted by the deputations of inserting new clauses at the last moment.

The minority bishops were not allowed to discuss the historical objections against papal infallibility with the deputation on the faith."[211] In a letter Bishop Le Courtier complains, 'See what more than aught else destroys our liberty: it is crushed under the respect we have for our Head.'[212] Later in frustrated anger, Bishop Francois Le Courtier tossed his council documents into the river Tiber and left Rome. The papers were retrieved and brought to the attention of Vatican officials. The price for this gesture was extracted three years later, when he was dismissed as Bishop of Montpellier.[213]

In spite of the unequal representation and Pius IX using the power and prestige of his office, there was still a large number - eighty-eight bishops - who voted against Papal Infallibility, which was enshrined in the constitution, *Pastor Aeternus.* Sixty- two bishops, many of whom were de facto opponents, voted with reservations, with only four hundred and fifty-one giving a clear yes - this is less than half of the one thousand and eighty four prelates with voting privileges and less than two-thirds of the seven hundred bishops in

---

211 The Triumph of the Holy See, page 156, Derek Holmes. Burns & Oates, London. 1978.

212 Butler, First Vatican Council, page 447.

213 Hasler, page 139.

attendance at the commencement of the Council. Over seventy-six bishops in Rome abstained from voting and fifty-five bishops informed the Pope that while maintaining their opposition to the definition that out of 'filial piety and reverence, which very recently brought our representatives to the feet of your Holiness, do not allow us in a cause so closely concerning Your Holiness to say 'non placet' (it is not pleasing) openly in the face of the Father.'[214] This statement alone speaks volumes for the subservience that these bishops had for the immense authority figure of the Pope – a presence unknown in the councils of the Early Church.

Thus lacking a moral unanimity or even a clear two-thirds majority, Papal Infallibility was now elevated as an article of faith equal to the Holy Trinity and the Incarnation. A belief that could not possibly meet the Vincentian canon of *Universality, Antiquity and Consent,* and in fact a belief not universally shared by Catholics even within living memory of the Council that solemnly defined it. Years later, Orthodox theologian Sergei Bulgakov, observed with disdain that, 'The Vatican Council has as much right to call itself a Council as today's meetings of delegates from the Soviet republics can claim to be a free expression of the will of the people.'[215]

---

214 Butler, The Vatican Council, page 408, 409.
215 Hasler, page 143.

CHAPTER IX

The Opposition

The most illustrious, best-educated bishops of the Church, filled the ranks of the opposition to Papal Infallibility and so great was their resistance that the Council had to employ closure. Cardinal Schwarzenberg, Archbishop of Prague and Rauscher, Archbishop of Vienna are sighted by Butler as being the leaders of the opposition: "They had proved themselves pillars of the Church.....Rauscher was a man of wide erudition, especially in patrology. On arrival in Rome for the Council he was greeted with universal respect, and hailed as one of the glories of the Council."[216] Cardinal Schwarzenberg, in his written observations stated that, Scriptural texts used to prove personal infallibility were deficient and that the Church Fathers taught that infallibility was not possible apart from the Council of bishops.[217]

The greatest opposition came from Germany and Austria, joined by all the Hungarian bishops headed by the Primate of Hungary, Simor, Archbishop of Esztergom and Haynald, Archbishop of Kaloesa, "Both of them learned theologians and apostolic bishops, they were conspicuous as two of the best Latin orators at the Council."[218] Prominent in this group was Joseph Karl

216 Butler, page 109.
217 Friedrich, Vol. ii, page 221.
218 Ibid., page 111.

Hefele, Professor at the University of Tubingen and now Bishop of Rottenburg, whom Dom. Butler describes as, "perhaps the most learned bishop of the Council in the domain of Church history and patrology. His *History of the Councils* is the classical work on the subject."[219]

In a speech Butler describes as, "Probably the most impressive adverse speech,"[220] he dismisses the Biblical verses such as Luke 22:32 used to support the claims of infallibility. "In short the doctrine of infallibility of the Roman Pontiff does not seem to me to be based on Holy Scripture or on ecclesiastical tradition. Altogether to the contrary; unless I am mistaken, Christian antiquity obstructs the doctrine, and a few doubts against the declaration of the new dogma arise from Church history and the words of the holy Fathers." He reminded the assembled bishops that when controversies arose in the Early Church, it was the Vincentian canon of *Universality, Antiquity and Consent,* that was appealed to. "No one ever imagined that there was the short cut of obtaining an infallible decision on a controversy from any one single individual." To this Hefele gave examples such as the conflicting dogmatic decrees of Pope Vigilius and other Popes, the writings of the Greek and Latin Fathers that are completely incompatible with the notion of Papal Infallibility.[221]

Turning to the Council of Chalcedon he said: "If ever there was an *ex cathedra* dogmatic document it was

219 The Vatican Council, 1869 - 1870, page 110, Dom. Cuthbert Butler, Collins and Harvill Press, London, 1962.
220 Ibid., page 307.
221 Documenta, Friedrich, Vol. ii, page 220.

Leo's Letter to Flavian. But, at the Council all the bishops were called on to declare on oath if it was conformable to the Creeds of Nicaea and Constantinople; therefore, they were called on to judge of its orthodoxy and the Fathers of the Council subjected the Letter to an examination as to its orthodoxy. It was not said to the bishops, 'Here is a dogmatic letter of the Pope; hear it, and submit'; but rather, 'Hear it, and judge'. Some of the bishops thought it in three places subject of heresy; but no one said they were temerarious for doubting; no one questioned their right to doubt. And so a four fold argument against papal infallibility can be drawn from Chalcedon."[222] He then turned to the damaging evidence of Pope Honorius' condemnation for heresy by the Sixth Ecumenical Council. In protesting that infallibility was not a revealed doctrine of the Church, Bishop Hefele said: 'I yield to no one in reverence for the Apostolic See and the Holy Father: but I do not think it lawful to proceed to a declaration of the infallibility. Bishops are witnesses, not arbiters of the Faith.'[223]

Joseph Georg Strossmayer, Bishop of Bosnia and Sirmium was a candid unflinching witness for the minority. Amidst a storm of protest, Strossmayer complained against the decision to pass acts by majority vote. He reminded the Council that dogma can only be imposed by a moral unanimity: "In the recent Regulation it is laid down that questions are to be settled

222 Butler, page 306.
223 Ibid., pages 306, 307.

by a majority of votes. Against this some bishops have put in a statement, asking if the ancient rule of moral unanimity.....". His words were drowned out by the uproar and when he attempted to continue the bishops started to leave their seats: "He is Lucifer, anathema, anathema!.....He is another Luther let him be cast out!"[224] Following this uproarious meeting one of the American bishops said to Lord Acton; "There is certainly one assembly in the world rougher than the American Congress."[225]

Felix Dupanloup, Bishop of Orleans was, "one of the most outstanding figures of the period and the Council..... As Rector of the Episcopal college of Paris, he raised it to the very first rank among the colleges and lycees of France." Felix Dupanloup, "soon became the chief Catholic champion in all public controversies, the recognized spokesman of the bishops, the most prominent bishop in France, and one of the most prominent bishops of the whole Catholic world."[226] Dupanloup stated publicly that a definition of infallibility was inopportune; that an accurate definition was impossible and would only serve to alienate non Catholic Christians."[227]

Another leading French prelate was Georges Darboy, the brilliant Archbishop of Paris, who

---

224 Ibid, page 237, 238.

225 The First Council of the Vatican, page 147, James J. Hennesey, S.J. Herder and Herder, New York, 1963.

226 Ibid., page 51.

227 The Triumph of the Holy See, page 153, Derek Holmes, Burns & Oates, London, 1978.

following the Council was executed by the Paris Communards and died blessing his executioners. Darboy held that Papal Infallibility could neither be supported by history or common sense[228] and that it could only be passed, "with the moral unanimity of the Council: should there be a substantial minority the validity and authority of the Council will be exposed to doubt."[229]

There was Henri Maret, Bishop of Sura, dean of the theological faculty of the Sorbonne. This bishop whom Butler describes as, "a learned and able man of high character",[230] published a two volume work, *Du Concile generale et de la paix religieuse,* which he claimed would destroy the notion of Papal Infallibility. The French ambassador presented a copy to Pius IX and copies were sent to every Catholic bishop. In his book Maret claims, "the supreme authority of a General Council over the Pope even in matters of Faith" and strongly denies the personal infallibility of the Pope.[231] Of Pope Honorius he writes, "A pope whose doctrine and whose person are condemned by three General Councils, as by his successors, evidently possess neither absolute sovereignty nor infallibility."

From England William Clifford, Bishop of Clifton and Archbishop George Errington represented the minority. At an audience with Pius IX in front of his fellow clerics, Pius accused Clifford of opposing him

---

228 Ibid., page 153.
229 Butler, page 308.
230 Ibid., page 98.
231 Ibid., page 98.

because he had been, "passed over" for the post of Archbishop of Westminster.[232] The Irish bishops were John McHale, Archbishop of Tuam and Bishops Moriarty of Kerry, Furlong of Ferns and Leahy of Dromore.

NORTH AMERICAN OPPOSITION AND THE ANXIETY OF ENGLAND'S JOHN HENRY NEWMAN

From North America the opposing bishops were Archbishops McCloskey of New York, Kenrick of St. Louis, Purcell of Cincinnati, Connolly of Halifax and nineteen U. S. bishops. The scrappy, humorous Augustin Verot, Bishop of Savannah and *enfant terrible* of the Council, told the assembled bishops that Acts 11, did not reveal that Christians were taught the infallibility of Peter by the Apostles; if they had, they never would have contended with him. Paul certainly knew nothing of Peter's infallibility when he, "withstood him to his face because he was to be blamed." Gal. 11:11. "It is true" he went on, "that the Irish believe in the Pope's infallibility; but they also believe in their priests' infallibility.....But will the Cardinal of Dublin say that they believe (Pope) Hadrian IV was infallible when he handed over Ireland to the King of England!"[233] He then remarked that all the

232 How the Pope Became Infallible, page 85, August Bernhard Hasler, Doubleday and Co., Inc., Garden City, New York, 1981.

233 Butler, page 311, 312..

armed might of Britain had not been able to force the Fenians to accept that gift as an accomplished fact.[234]

Thomas Connolly, Capuchin Archbishop of Halifax, Nova Scotia, arrived in Rome as a convinced infallibilist, however, after studying the arguments pro and con, he became a staunch opponent. He admitted, that he would have preferred to have continued believing in Papal Infallibility and so challenged his fellow infallibilist bishops, to produce a good argument from the first three hundred years of the Church. Since no convincing arguments were forthcoming, this sporting prelate offered one thousand pounds, (about thirty thousand dollars U.S. today) to whoever could produce convincing evidence. All he received for his offer were spurious texts.[235]

Michael Domenec, Bishop of Pittsburgh told the Council: "…..that the proposed dogma would spell nothing but disaster in the land where he had labored for over thirty years. Bishops like John England, John Hughes, and Francis Patrick Kenrick had always silenced Protestant attacks by declaring that papal infallibility was not a Catholic dogma, and that no Catholic was bound to hold it. Now, continued Domenec, if infallibility is proclaimed to be a dogma, the bishops would have to return to their pulpits and retract the charge of calumny that they had made against

234 Hennesey, page 236.
235 Hasler, page l53.

the Protestants. The definition, he said, would make liars out of them."[236]

The Irish born Peter Richard Kenrick, Archbishop of St. Louis, was one of the most unflinching opponents of the definition and when the Council voted for closure, he had the speech he was unable to deliver, published in Naples. This speech encompassing one hundred pages is a powerful, sweeping indictment of Papal Infallibility; a concept Kenrick insists, has no support in Scripture, history or tradition:

> I boldly declare that the opinion, as set down in the *schema,* is not a doctrine of faith, and that it cannot become such by any definition whatsoever, even of a council. We are custodians of the deposit of faith, not its masters. We are teachers of the faithful entrusted to our care just in so far as we are witnesses.[237]

Regarding the lack of Scriptural and patristic evidence for the definition, Kenrick asserts that the constant teaching of the Church is that Scriptural interpretation cannot be contrary to the unanimous consent of the Church Fathers. Kenrick said that in the Bull of Boniface VIII, *Unam Sanctam*, the Church claimed the right to depose Christian Sovereigns yet, "down to the beginning of the seventeenth century - for four whole centuries - this definition of the papal power seems to have been in force, and was said even by the

---

236 Hennesey, page 242.
237 Kenrick (Naples edition) page 40.

most learned theologians of the seventeenth century to be a matter of faith.....The church, then, through all that period seems to have approved by its assent the bull *Unam Sanctam,* hardly a single bishop having objected to it.....The tacit assent of the bishops, therefore, for no less than four centuries, did not have the effect to constitute the opinion of the power of the pope in temporals into a doctrine of the Catholic faith, which is obvious of itself, since otherwise the rejection of it now would be equivalent to defection from the unity of the Catholic church."[238]

On the tradition of the Irish Church Kenrick observed, that while most of them now believe the Pope to be infallible, it had not always been so. It had not been a doctrine taught at Maynooth, (Seminary) until Father John O'Hanlon proposed it in 1831 as a theory for discussion.[239]

England's Reverend John Henry Newman (later made Cardinal), wrote a letter to Bishop Ullathorne on January 28, 1870 in which he agonizes over the historical difficulties of Papal Infallibility for, "I look with anxiety at the prospect of having to defend decisions which may not be difficult to my private judgment, but may be most difficult to maintain logically in face of historical facts."[240]

---

238 Friedrich Documenta , Vol. I, page 204 – 206.
239 Kenrick, page 49 - 56.
240 Butler, page 182.

CHAPTER IX

UNIATE'S RIGHTS ARE INFRINGED

In 1867 a bull *Reversus,* was proclaimed by Pius IX, that directly infringed on the customs and privileges of the Uniate's (Eastern Christians in union with Rome). This bull now demanded papal confirmation of all episcopal and patriarchal appointments. It was therefore, under the cloud of this bull that Uniate bishops made their way to the First Vatican Council with, "minds full of forebodings of what might be in store for their privileges, customs, and even their rites."[241]

The seventy-eight year old Chaldean Patriarch, Joseph Audu, became their chief spokesman and on January 25th, 1870, he brought these concerns to the Council in a speech. The following day a terrible, scandalous scene took place at the Vatican. Pope Pius IX, upon hearing of Audu's opposition to his bull, summoned him and as soon as he appeared in the papal chambers, the Pope bolted the door. According to Bishop Felix Dupanloup, the Pope warned the aging Patriarch that he would never get out until he had signed the contents of the bull *Reversus*. "While the Patriarch remained outwardly calm, the Pope was trembling with rage. Audu had only two alternatives: to resign or submit. Out of fear he chose the second. Later on, however, further conflicts arose between Pope and Patriarch, and finally Pius IX removed him from office."[242] This deplorable piece of drama, caused quite

241 Ibid., page 193.
242 Hasler, page 89.

a stir among the bishops adding further proof that this was not a free Council. Archbishop Georges Darboy, described it as a, "robber synod". "Under such circumstances many bishops were afraid to speak their mind. Some of them, especially Eastern bishops, left the Council before it ended. Pius IX encouraged the departure of such 'Gallican troublemakers.' 'Right - thinking' bishops, on the other hand, were detained in Rome."[243]

ENGLAND'S LORD ACTON - A SCATHING WITNESS

The most distinguished Catholic layman of his day, who strenuously opposed Papal Infallibility, was England's John Emerich Edward Dalberg Acton, 8th Baronet and First Baron. This civilized, cosmopolitan, German trained historian, as Regius Professor of Modern History at Cambridge University, planned the twelve volume, *Cambridge Modern History*. To Lord Acton, Papal Infallibility was, "this great calamity", "this insane enterprise." His implacable opposition drew from Pius IX the scathing epithet, "that blackguard Actonuccio" (-uccio = ugly, nasty).[244]

Acton was in Rome for all but the last six weeks of the Council and so provided an excellent eyewitness. He describes in anguish, the ultramontane activity in

243 Ibid., page 89. Hasler provides another source for this incident: Robert Hotz, Das Malaise der Unierten. Nachwort zur Woche der christlichen Einheit, Orientierung, 42, 1978, 17.

244 Ibid., page 87.

which, "after Scripture had been subjugated, tradition itself was deposed; and the constant belief of the past yielded to the general conviction of the present. And, as antiquity had given way to universality, universality made way for authority. The Word of God and the authority of the Church came to be declared the two sources of religious knowledge. Divines of this school, after preferring the Church to the Bible, preferred the modern Church to the ancient, and ended by sacrificing both to the Pope.....Accordingly, the organ of one ultramontane bishop lately declared that infallibility could be defined without argument; and the Bishop of Nimes thought that the decision need not be preceded by long and careful discussion. The Dogmatic Commission of the Council proclaims that the existence of tradition has nothing to do with evidence, and that objections taken from history are not valid when contradicted by ecclesiastical decrees. Authority must conquer history."[245] .

Lord Acton writes that with the doctrine of Papal Infallibility came the inclination to bury embarrassing evidence, as was the suppression of the *Liber Diurnus* (see Chapter II). He scornfully relates: "When it was discovered in the manuscript of the *Liber Diurnus* that the Popes had for centuries condemned Honorius in their profession of faith, Cardinal Bona, the most eminent man in Rome, advised that the book should be suppressed if the difficulty could not be got over; and it was suppressed accordingly. Men guilty of this kind of

245 Essays on Freedom and Power, page 297, 298, Lord Acton, Meridian Book, Cleveland, Ohio, 1972.

fraud would justify it by saying that their religion transcends the wisdom of philosophers, and cannot submit to the criticism of historians."[246]

On the eve of the Council, two books were published that were damaging to the theory of Papal Infallibility. England's John Henry Newman, who was later to become Cardinal under Pope Leo XIII, suggested to Egyptologist and theologian Sir Peter Le Page Renouf, that he write a study of Pope Honorius I (625-638), who suffered condemnation for heresy by the Sixth Ecumenical Council Renouf concluded that Pope Honorius had indeed counseled heresy and was therefore justly condemned. On December 14th, 1868 his book, *The Condemnation of Pope Honorius* was placed on the Index of Forbidden Books.

The other book was written by German historian Johan Josef Ignaz von Dollinger entitled, *The Pope and the Council* (Published under the Pseudonym "Janus"). This book was also quickly placed on the Index of Forbidden Books on November 26, 1869, and to make sure that this book would not see the light of day in Catholic circles, the decree stressed, *quocumque idiomate*, "in whatever language" it may be published. [247]

[246] Acton, page 298.
[247] Hasler, page 62.

CHAPTER IX

MANNING OF ENGLAND - THE COUNCIL ZEALOT

The anti-historical bias of the Council found its champion in England's Archbishop, (later Cardinal) Henry Edward Manning, chief whip of the infallibilists. This Oxford educated, gaunt, austere looking man had worked in the British Colonial Office before being ordained to the Anglican priesthood. In 1832 he was profoundly affected by the death of his wife. After a period of spiritual turmoil he was received into the Roman Catholic Church in 1851. The least commendable facet of Manning's character - employing back room politics to achieve his ends, was offset by his genuine devotion to the needs of poor Catholic children. His reputation at winning converts was legendary.

Manning was openly hostile to historians and historical criticism that he viewed as destructive to the faith. He stated scornfully: "It is time, for historical science and the scientific historians, with all their arrogance, to be thrust back into their proper sphere, to be kept within their proper limits. And this Council will do just that, not with controversies and condemnations but with the words, 'it has pleased the Holy Spirit and us'." Manning obviously had Ignaz von Dollinger and the historical school in mind. "For Manning, once the Church had spoken, all historical problems were liquidated. The Holy Spirit, he believed, was so closely allied with the Church that errors or false steps were impossible; and this faith gave him utter certainty. The story goes - and it seems quite believable - that Manning and his circle had a motto, 'Dogma must triumph over history,' or 'Dogma has conquered history.'

Bishop Felix Dupanloup, reports a similar remark from the no less intransigent suffragan bishop of Geneva, Gaspare Mermillod that, 'Infallibility sets the nations free from history.'[248] Archbishop Peter Kenrick of St. Louis, remarked to Manning (a convert to Catholicism) that he reminded him of, "what used to be said of the English settlers in Ireland, that they were more Irish than the Irish. 'The Most Reverend Archbishop', he found to be 'certainly more Catholic than any Catholic whom I have ever known.' Manning, he declared, had no doubt about the personal, separate, and absolute infallibility of the pope, and he did not intend to allow anyone else to have any doubts about it. Rather he was like a prophet who took care to see to it that his predictions came true."[249]

THE AGONY OF DR. VON DOLLINGER

Johan Josef Ignaz von Dollinger (1799-1890), was Germany's greatest Roman Catholic historian. He was professor of canon law and Church history at Munich University and was president of the Bavarian Royal Academy of Sciences. Under his leadership, Munich University was to gain first place in Europe as a centre for ecclesiastical studies and Butler said that von Dollinger was, "the greatest champion of the Catholic

248 Ibid., page 179.
249 Hennesey, page 247.

cause in Germany."[250] His contemporaries regarded him as one of the greatest historical scholars in Europe.

His book, *The Pope and the Council*, is a frontal attack on Papal Infallibility. Dollinger claims that this notion was completely unknown in the Early Church and has always been relentlessly resisted by the Orthodox Church, therefore, he says: "to the adherents of the theory of infallibility the history of the Church must appear as an incomprehensible problem." For no one was ever accused of heresy in denying the authority of the popes in their pronouncements of faith, and it was only much later, with the assistance of a good number of forgeries, i.e. the Decretals of Pseudo-Isidore etc., that Papal Infallibility gained ground.

Before the Council convened, he wrote to Bishop Johan Baptist Greith: "Before I could ever inscribe this modern invention (Papal Infallibility) on the tablet of my mind, I would first have to plunge my fifty years of theological, historical, and patristic studies into Lethe (river of forgetfulness) and then draw them forth like a blank sheet of paper."[251]

When Papal Infallibility was declared a dogma of the Roman Catholic Church, Dollinger was requested by his bishop to offer his submission on March 28, 1871. He replied in a letter to the Archbishop of Munich and requested a hearing before a Board of bishops, theologians and "the most eminent German historians of the Catholic faith." Dollinger further tells the

250 Butler, page 433.
251 Hasler, page 180.

Archbishop he prepared to prove that, "The new articles of faith rest for their establishment from the Scriptures on the passages Matt. XVI.18, John XXI.17, and as far as the infallibility is concerned on the passage Luke XXII.32, with which, biblically considered, it stands and falls. Now we are bound by a solemn oath, which I have taken twice, not to accept or expound the Scriptures 'in any other way than according to the unanimous agreement of the Fathers.' The Fathers of the Church have all without exception expounded the passages in question in a sense entirely different from the new Decree, and especially in the passage Luke XXII.32 they were far from seeing an infallibility granted to all the Popes."[252] He then states that Papal Infallibility rests, "on a complete misunderstanding of ecclesiastical tradition in the first thousand years of the Church, and on a distortion of her history; it contradicts the clearest facts and evidences."[253]

Dollinger then offers to prove, "in public, that two General Councils and several popes as early as the fifteenth century decided the question of the extent of the pope's power and infallibility by solemn decrees which were proclaimed by the Council, and repeatedly confirmed by the popes, and that the Decrees of the 18th July, 1870 stand in glaring contradiction to these Resolutions, whence it is impossible that they should be binding."[254]

---

252 Declarâtions and Letters on the Vatican Decrees, 1869 - 1887, page 83, 84, Ignaz von Dollinger, T & T Clark, Edinburgh, 1891.

253 Ibid., page 84.

254 Ibid., page 85.

He then reminds his bishops that, "On a former occasion your Grace honoured my book on the earliest, i.e. the Apostolic Age of the Church with your approval, and in Germany generally it was regarded on the Catholic side as a faithful picture of the times of the Church's foundation; even from Jesuit and Ultramontane circles no important censure has been expressed. But if the new Decrees contain the truth, then I shall be met with the reproach of having perverted the history of the apostles. The whole portion of my book on the constitution of the earliest Church, and my representation of the relation in which Paul and the rest of the apostles stood to Peter, are in that case thoroughly false, and I should have to condemn my own book, and confess that I have never understood either St. Luke's Acts of the Apostles or the Apostolic Epistles."[255]

After offering the bishops a comprehensive, detailed explanation for not submitting and again pleading for a public hearing he ends his letter, "As a Christian, as theologian, as historian, as citizen, I cannot accept this doctrine."[256] The Church denied him the right to plead his cause, something it allowed Martin Luther to do, as they did with Hus and Jerome at the Council of Constance and a whole host of men who ran afoul of church doctrine. Dollinger was excommunicated on April 23rd. 1871 when he was 72 years old. He died at the age of 90 on January 10th, 1890.

---

[255] Ibid., page 91.
[256] Ibid., page 103.

In the intervening years between his excommunication and death, many efforts were made to gain his submission in letters and interviews, but always to no avail. Perhaps the most poignant and revealing correspondence, is the exchange between himself and 'A Lady of High Rank', who implored him from the depths of her heart to save himself from eternal damnation. In a kind, courteous reply, Dollinger wrote: "I am now in my eighty-first year, and was a public teacher of theology for forty-seven years, during which long period no censure, nor even a challenge that I should defend myself or make a better explanation, has ever reached me from ecclesiastical dignitaries either at home or abroad. I had *never* taught the new Articles of Faith advanced by Pius IX and his Council. In my youth, when I studied at Bamberg and Wurzburg, they were regarded as theological opinions, and many added 'ill founded' opinions.....Then came the fatal year 1870. If I had obeyed the summons to affirm the new dogmas on oath, I should there by have declared myself to have been an heretical teacher, and not only myself, but also my deceased teachers, as also a number of friends and colleagues who found themselves in the same position. It was in vain that I begged they would let me remain by the faith and confession to which I had hitherto been faithful without blame and without contradiction. Yesterday still orthodox, I was today a heretic worthy of excommunication, not because I had changed my teaching, but because others had considered it advisable to undertake the alteration, and to make opinions into Articles of Faith. I ought, as the favourite expression of the Jesuits runs, 'to make a sacrifice of my intellect' (*sacrificio dell intellecto*). This is what your Ladyship also demands of me. But if I did so, in a question which is for me the historical eye perfectly clear and unambiguous, there would then no longer be for me any such thing as historical truth and certainty; I should then have to suppose that my whole life long I had been in a world of dizzy illusion, and that in historical matters I am altogether incapable of distinguishing truth from fable and falsehood."

He then informs her that an oath would be a double perjury because I would have to, "break the oath which was laid upon me on my entrance upon my official duties - the oath, namely, always to expound the Holy Scriptures in agreement with the interpretation of the holy Fathers; and, second, in the required oath I should have to carry out a moral self-destruction on myself. For with this oath I should testify that I had been teaching erroneous doctrines all my life, and that I had falsely understood and misinterpreted the history of the Church, the Fathers, and the Bible. And what should I gain thereby? First, I should not have another peaceful hour for the rest of my life, and then I should pass into the other world as a liar, laden with the fearful burden of perjury…."[257]

Dollinger's prominence in the Church is attested by the numerous appeals made to him. On his eightieth birthday, the Archbishop of Munich informs him that the Pope is as earnest for his return as he is; for the Pope, "would so gladly stretch out the hand of peace to

---

257 Ibid., pages 131 - 134.

you. May God in His goodness grant that this moment may arrive before the day draws nearer to its close and the night cometh, - to the joy of thousands who, like myself, are yearning for it, and to the consolation of the Holy Church….."[258]

EXCOMMUNICATIONS, SEVERING OF TIES AND CRUMBLING OPPOSITION

Even after the definition passed, many professors continued to focus on the enormous historical difficulties that stood in the way of the definition. Shortly after the Council closed, twenty professors of theology and clerical teachers of philosophy were excommunicated in Germany and Austria for refusing submission.

Unable to reconcile Papal Infallibility with the historical record, two-thirds of all Catholic historians teaching at German Universities severed their ties with the Church. In other countries theologians and historians left the Church for the same reasons.[259] It is argued that Papal Infallibility would face an even stiffer challenge now, due to a greater abundance of historical text. Hence, it is highly unlikely that a General Council of the Church would pass it if it were put to a vote today.

The resistance of the bishops crumbled and one by one they made their submission. For the more stubborn

[258] Ibid., page 138.
[259] Hasler, page 227.

prelates, like Church historian Joseph Karl Hefele Bishop of Rottenburg, Rome applied steady, increasing pressure, by withholding application for marriage dispensations.[260] Eventually, Hefele like his fellow bishops cracked and he made his *sacrificio dell intellecto* (the sacrifice of his intellect), "casting my own subjectivity at the feet of the supreme ecclesiastical authority."

Lord Acton wrote of these bishops, "But it was certain that there were men amongst them who would renounce their belief rather than incur the penalty of excommunication, who preferred authority to proof, and accepted the Pope's declaration, 'La tradizione son' io.', (I am tradition)."[261]

260 Ibid., page 435.
261 Acton, page 327.

CHAPTER X

A Choice of Paths

At the Randwick Racetrack in Sydney Australia, a huge papal mass celebrated the beatification of Mother Mary MacKillop, an Australian nun who founded the Sisters of St. Joseph. The description of this event is mostly taken from the *Catholic Weekly*, March 5th, 1995, the official journal of the Archdiocese of Sydney Australia, as it appeared in the traditional Catholic *The Latin Mass* magazine.[262]

Nuns attired in snappy business suits participated in the procession to the altar and then assisted Pope John Paul II, as acolytes and ministers. Dancing girls performed, "using rhythmical movements of hands, and feet and head, together with the swaying of the body." In spite of the presence of large numbers of priests available to distribute Holy Communion, laymen were given ciboria containing unconsecrated bread which were then elevated at the offertory: "Thus laymen and women were involved in the central mystery of the Eucharist more closely than they've ever been before."

That ancient proclamation of faith, the Nicene Creed, was replaced by an "interesting question and answer format." The traditional penitential rite was supplanted by "the incorporation of an Aboriginal tribal ritual into the liturgy of the Mass itself. The 'smoking

---

262 The Latin Mass, Vol. 4, no. 3, Summer 1995, page 32 - 34, Foundation for Catholic Reform, Fort Collins, Colorado.

ceremony' became part of the Mass - another first!" This interesting ritual featured a man walking with an oil drum containing a bed of hot coals, accompanied by a woman who occasionally sprinkled gum leaves on the coals.

The offertory was also not without interest, consisting of a ritual called "Gathering of the Soils", accompanied by repeated references to the "soil, sun, sea, elements which in spite of urbanization are buried deep in the Australian psyche". Soil was solemnly offered by the Sisters of St. Joseph from the various countries they operated in.

For those Catholics holding serious reservations about this strange liturgy, there are soothing words of assurance, that "every detail of the papal ceremonies celebrated here was approved well in advance by the Holy Father's Master of Ceremonies.....Be assured that nothing could be or was sprung upon the Holy Father. Everything had prior Vatican approval." The *Catholic Weekly*, simply gushes in self congratulatory enthusiasm now that Australia has been placed on the liturgical map:

> As time goes on it will be referred to as a 'liturgical breakthrough,' not only here in Australia but in the worldwide Church. It will be quoted in liturgical manuals and articles as an important milestone in appropriate liturgical development and adaptation. It will be looked upon as a benchmark indicating what is permissible and desirable in good liturgy.....Randwick has changed the benchmark of

> liturgical correctness; the ante has been pushed up; individuals and groups are now challenged to adjust. The Vatican liturgical watchdog has turned out to be more liberal and progressive than was thought.....Now it's (sic) the local Church has some catching up to do.

Yet some thirteen years prior to this it is interesting to note, that in answer to a question regarding liturgical dance the Sacred Congregation for the Sacraments and Divine Worship, issued a reply on January 8th, 1982, quoting from its official journal *Notitiae*, XI, 1975, pp. 202-205, stating that:

> Hence it is not possible to introduce something of that sort in the liturgical celebrations: It would mean to bring into the liturgy one of the most desacralized and desacralizing elements; and this would be seen as introducing an atmosphere of profanity.....Nor is it acceptable to introduce into the Liturgy the so-called artistic ballet because it would reduce the liturgy to mere entertainment.....

However; liturgical dance now has official Vatican approval - it is very popular in Latin America - as do other practices that were once condemned by the Holy See, i.e. communion in the hand, altar girls etc. In fact liturgical dance is now officially recorded - in Latin - in article 42 of the new Vatican document, *The Roman Liturgy and Inculturation.* There is something slightly comic in dignifying this sort of nonsense by solemnly recording it in Latin; e.g. approval is giving to hand clapping, "…..manuum percussio….." and rhythmic swaying of the body, "…..fluctuationes rhythmicae….." etc. When Pope John Paul II reaffirmed the Church's historic ban on female altar servers in *Inaestimabile Donum*, in 1980 it was this same official Vatican journal, *Notitiae* that reassured the Catholic world that:

> (the) general discipline of the Church (against female altar servers) has been set in stone by canon 44 of the Collection of Laodicea which dates generally from the end of the 4th century and which has figured in almost all canonical collections of East and West.[263]

The above news item on the Papal Mass at Randwick was chosen because, I think it is both symbolic and symptomatic of the Roman Catholic Church today. Sadly, the Roman Catholic Church has lost her traditional moorings and this loss is very evident in the first place you would expect to find it, i.e. in the Mass which is her spiritual heart. Rome's problems have been structural since she broke with the Eastern Church and developed a highly centralized sovereign Papal Monarchy. The enormous political upheavals and numerous wars that resulted from papal temporal claims and the separation of the Eastern Church, the Great Schism, the Protestant Revolt and now this crisis the Catholic Church is undergoing today, which many observers claim to be the worst crisis in her history, are problems of structure.

---

263 Ibid., Vol. 4, No. 4, page 44, Fall 1995.

A SINGLE MONARCHICAL BISHOP FAILS TO PRESERVE STABILITY AND TRADITION

Rome abandoned the collegial form of government that is intrinsic to the very nature of Christianity, adopting instead a single authoritarian monarchy that has failed to supply the stability and strength of a collegial model. One only has to look at the enormous swings Roman Catholics have had to endure in their liturgy in the last one hundred years. The Mass was so rigidly controlled that, "even as late as 1857 the prohibition to translate the Ordinary of the Mass, (into the vernacular from Latin) was renewed by Pope Pius IX." Pope Leo XIII only removed it from the Index of Forbidden Books in 1897.[264]

Compare this mindset with the Papal Mass at the Randwick racetrack - they are universes apart. It was the capricious act of one sovereign Roman Pontiff, Paul VI that caused the liturgical revolution, which is still ongoing with Pope John Paul II officially sanctioning altar girls and liturgical dance. The use of altar girls has been ranked as one of the most radical, revolutionary, liturgical changes in the history of the Church.

In the rich symbolic language of the liturgy, altar boys vested in cassocks and surplices were a reflection of the male priesthood. In fact, assisting the priest at the altar is not only the initial step on the road to the priesthood, but in the past, has proven to be a rich

---

264 The Mass of the Roman Rite, Its Origins and Development, Vol. l, page 161, Joseph A. Jungmann, S.J. Christian Classics, Inc. Westminster, Maryland. 1992.

source of vocations. Vested female altar servers has severed an ancient tradition of the Church and in the symbolic language of the liturgy, it has communicated an ambiguous, uncertain message regarding Rome's ultimate commitment to a male priesthood.

Given the conciliar government of the Orthodox Church, such massive swings in liturgical practice - not to mention some of the wilder aberrations - would be incomprehensible. Roman Catholic apologists' claim that a Supreme Pontiff, speaking with an authoritative voice, is necessary for the preservation of doctrine and tradition and it is only this that provides them with a rock of certitude. However, I would suggest that in the nine hundred years since Rome and the Orthodox Church separated, it is the Orthodox Church that has provided the greater witness to the liturgical and dogmatic traditions of the Early Church.

This contention is supported in an amazingly candid article that appeared in *The Latin Mass* (a traditional Roman Catholic magazine) entitled *Keeping the Faith When the Church is in Chaos.* The author is Count Neri Caponi, an Italian Catholic aristocrat, who consults for the archdiocese of Florence in canon law and has served as advocate to the Roman Rota and the Apostolic Signatura.

In his article, Count Caponi after addressing the various crises that have occurred in the Church, makes the point that the post-Vatican II Church in some ways, is in a worse state of crisis than the Church experienced during the Arian heresy that rocked the Church in the fourth century. He lays the blame of this at the feet of Pope Paul VI. His main reasons are that, "The principle vehicle of the faith, the liturgy was untouched by the Arian crisis" and that the current crisis has its origins and momentum from within the Church herself. However, continues Caponi all is not lost for there is a "branch of the Universal Church that has been mostly spared the infection of heresy. I refer to the Eastern Churches, both those in communion with Rome and those that are not. No one has dared to tamper with the Eastern liturgy in the Catholic Church - first because the Eastern Catholics are a minority and therefore thought to be less important by heretics in high places; and second, because it would have confirmed the worst suspicions of the Orthodox churches about Vatican tyranny and duplicity, and put an end to the ecumenical dialogue. Furthermore, there would have been an impressive exodus of Eastern faithful to the Orthodox churches. It is interesting to note that in the Roman Catholic cathedral of Athens, Greece, a sign warns, 'In this church Communion is *not* given in the hand.' Such a notice, I believe, may be found in most Latin churches in Orthodox countries." The reason for this prohibition he explains is that it would scandalize the Orthodox. He finally observes that because of their close association with Orthodox conservatism, "Eastern Catholic clerics are generally less prone to accept the heresies connected with foolish biblical studies, and instead adhere more faithfully to Christian dogma."[265]

---

[265] The Latin Mass, Vol. 3, No.2, page 29, 30, March/April 1994, Foundation for Catholic Reform, Fort Collins, Colorado.

CHAPTER X

UNION WITH ROME - CAN A WIDENING CHASM BE BRIDGED?

One of the great aims of Pope John Paul II is the unification of Rome and the Orthodox Church and this is best expressed in his encyclical, *Ut Unum Sint*, (That They May Be One) issued on May 25th, 1995. In this encyclical he quotes from the *Second Vatican Councils Decree on Ecumenism* when he says; "Contact with this glorious tradition is the most fruitful for the Church. As the Council points out;" 'From their very origins the Churches of the East have had a treasury from which the Church of the West has amply drawn for its liturgy, spiritual tradition and jurisprudence.' Pope John Paul makes the claim that the unity of the Church was, "maintained within those same structures through the Bishops, Successors of the Apostles, in communion with the Bishop of Rome. If today at the end of the second millennium we are seeking to restore full communion, it is to that unity, thus structured, that we must look." After relating the state of relations and on going dialogue with other separated Churches, John Paul gives the usual Scriptural proofs for Rome's supremacy and then explains that union with Rome will involve submitting to an authority, that is both exacting and comprehensive, in that it encompasses every facet of Church life:

> With the power and the authority without which such an office would be illusory, the Bishop of Rome must ensure the communion of all the Churches. For this reason, he is the first servant of

> unity. This primacy is exercised on various levels, including vigilance over the handing down of the Word, the celebration of the Liturgy and the Sacraments, the Church's mission, discipline and Christian life. It is the responsibility of the Successor of Peter to recall the requirements of the common good of the Church, should anyone be tempted to overlook it in the pursuit of personal interests. He has the duty to admonish, to caution and to declare at times that this or that opinion being circulated is irreconcilable with the unity of faith.

Pope John Paul then explains that unity with Rome also involves accepting Papal Infallibility: "He can also - under very specific conditions clearly laid down by the First Vatican Council - declare *ex cathedra* that a certain doctrine belongs to the deposit of faith."

Thus unification would require that the Orthodox Church recognize Rome's complete, universal jurisdiction, including Papal Infallibility. For the Orthodox Church, which has resisted papal claims for the last fifteen hundred years, while vigorously defending the principles of collegiality as the traditional form of church government, such recognition is absolutely impossible. On the other hand, Rome has just as vigorously pursued a papal monarchy and was even willing to sacrifice unity with Eastern Christendom to achieve this end.

In viewing these two mutually exclusive models of church government, it is difficult to see how unity can be achieved. How does one create a synthesis out of a collegial structure and a monarchical bishop, claiming supreme power as an infallible instrument of God? The Early Church does not point to the office of a single bishop as the living tradition of the Church, but rather to an ecumenical consensus or collective conscience, which is best exemplified by the early general councils. It is this model of government that is intrinsic to the nature of the Church and it is this that supplies her with enduring strength and stability.

Roman Catholic historian, Leo Donald Davis S.J. concludes his book, *The First Seven Ecumenical Councils (325-787)*, with the thought that, "Perhaps in the interests of better relations with the Orthodox and Protestants, the time has come to reconsider the whole question and accept with them only the first seven great councils as the truly ecumenical pillars of the faith."[266] Leo Donald Davis' idea is a great one, however, I do not think Rome is about to adopt it any time soon, as she is still very much wedded to the idea of Papal Monarchy as witnessed by Pope John Paul II's encyclical *Ut Unum Sint.*

It is not my wish to be a Jeremiah, any more than it is to be a Polyanna, with God of course anything is possible, but in human terms, when the two Churches are viewed with a critical unsentimental eye, I am not optimistic about any future union. Furthermore, the

---

[266] The First Seven Ecumenical Councils (325-787), Their History and Theology, page 325. Leo Donald Davis, S.J., A Michael Glazier Book, The Liturgical Press, Collegeville, Minnesota. 1990.

divergent paths of the two great Churches of Christendom have widened since Vatican II, giving Christians a more clear cut choice, for while it is true that relations are more friendly, it is also true that on a spiritual level, with the new Mass and liturgical aberrations, they are moving further apart - the papal mass at Randwick being a more glaring example.

THE CHURCH OF THE APOSTLES AND MARTYRS

As I mentioned in the first chapter, the changes in the liturgy and the liturgical abuses were certainly not the reason for leaving Rome - they were merely the catalyst. Rather it was that the claims of the papacy, especially Papal Infallibility that could not be reconciled with the historical record, as examined in the preceding chapters. In many ways this has not been an easy book to write, largely because of my personal difficulty in criticizing a church which had so long held my allegiance.

There were times when I felt a certain self-conscious unease in refuting claims I once held to be true and also because I know it will bruise the sensibilities of Roman Catholic readers including many of my friends and acquaintances. However, this was a book I had to write. Christianity is the very essence of my being, all my views, opinions and experiences are filtered through a Christian consciousness. Thus for me to cross over from Roman Catholicism to the Orthodox Church in silence, was an impossibility. The writing of this book was for me an apologia, a catharsis, a statement that had to be made, a door that had to be closed on two years of searching and emotional upheaval.

The Roman Catholic reader must understand that it is Rome herself who initiates the debate, with her claims of jurisdiction over the Orthodox Church. In refuting these claims, I have attempted to be both charitable and forthright, relying on the historical record, much of which originates from the Roman Catholic Church herself.

My years of searching led me with absolute certitude to the Orthodox Church, which is truly the Christian heartland. Since our conversion, the great spiritual wellspring for my family has become the Divine Liturgy, in which the Orthodox Church has retained the early Christian sense of rejoicing in Christ's victory over death and sin and celebrating the beauty of God and His creation in her magnificent prayers and sacred music. Orthodoxy is a lived faith with morning and evening prayers and a rich daily calendar of saints, feast days, festal days and fasts that are woven like a tapestry throughout the year. "The Orthodox Church, regarding man as a unity of soul and body, has always insisted that the body must be trained and disciplined as well as the soul. Fasting and self-control are the first virtues, the mother, root, source, and foundation of all good."[267]

---

[267] The Orthodox Church, page 306, Timothy Ware, Penguin Books, 1973.

A CHOICE OF PATHS

The Orthodox Church is the Church of the Seven Ecumenical Councils; those giant foundations of the Christian faith, preserving the universality and catholicity of the Early Church and home for increasing numbers of converts from other Christian denominations. In fact the *Encyclopaedia Britannica Year Book for 1995 and 1996* lists the Orthodox Church as the fastest growing mainline church in North America.[268]

The Orthodox Church is not a nostalgic museum piece, but a living creative force that has kept faith with the Church of the Apostles and Martyrs. Since her birth at Pentecost, in spite of horrendous persecution under the Ottoman Turks and the Communists, she has proven a splendid enduring witness to Christian tradition, which she will zealously guard until the consummation of the world.

---

[268] Encyclopaedia Britannica,Year Book, 1995, page 275, 1996, page 298.

Recommended Reading

Cantor, Norman F. *Civilization of the Middle Ages.* Harper Perennial, New York, 1993

Chadwick, Henry. *The Early Church.* Penguin Books, Revised Edition 1993.

Davis, S. J. Leo Donald. *The Seven Ecumenical Councils (325-787): Their History and Theology.* Liturgical Press, Collegeville, Minnesota.

Hasler, August Bernhard. *How the Pope Became Infallible.* Doubleday and Co., Garden City, New York, 1981.

Herrin, Judith. *The Foundation of Christendom.* Princeton University Press, Princeton, New Jersey.

Meyendorff, John. *Imperial Unity and Christian Divisions: The Church 450-680 A.D.* St. Vladimir's Seminary Press, Crestwood, New York, 1989.

Morris, Colin. *The Papal Monarchy: The Western Church from 1050 to 1250.* Clarendon Press, Oxford, 1991.

Papadakas, Aristeides. *The Christian East and the Rise of the Papacy.* St. Vladimir's Seminary Press, Crestwood, New York, 1994.

Robinson, I. S. *The Papacy 1073-1193.* Cambridge University Press, 1993.

RECOMMENDED READING

Runciman, Sir. Stever. *The Eastern Schism: A Study of the Eastern Churches During the XIIth and XIIth Centuries.* Oxford at the Clarendon Press, 1956.

Tierney, Brian. *Origins of Papal Infallibility 1150-1350: A Study on the Concepts of Infallibility, Sovereignty and Tradition in the Middle Ages. From the Series: Studies in the History of Christian Thought.* E. J. Brill, Leiden, Netherlands, 1972.

INDEX

A

B

INDEX

INDEX

INDEX

INDEX

I

J

K

L

INDEX

INDEX

INDEX

R

INDEX

S

T

U

INDEX

BUY 5 OR MORE ITEMS GET A 40% DISCOUNT

YES! YOU CAN MIX AND MATCH ANY ITEMS!

BOOKS

TWO PATHS Michael Whelton $22.95 (With 4 items) $13.77

Papal Monarchy Versus Collegial Tradition. Catholic or Orthodox, what is the true church?

THE SCANDAL OF GENDER Patrick Mitchell $22.95 (With 4 items) $13.77

The teachings of the Fathers on the role of women and men in the Church.

ETERNAL DAY** Seth Farber **$22.95 (With 4 items) $13.77

The Orthodox alternative to modern psychology

THE WAY** Clark Carlton **$22.95 (With 4 items) $13.77

What every Protestant should know about the Orthodox Church.

THE FAITH** Clark Carlton **$22.95 (With 4 items) $13.77

The best Orthodox catechism and study guide available. Endorsed by all Orthodox jurisdictions.

LETTERS TO FR. A** Frank Schaeffer **$22.95 (With 4 items) $13.77

How to be Orthodox in modern America.

DANCING ALONE** Frank Schaeffer **$20. (With 4 items) $12.00

The best selling story of personal journey of conversion.

SAVING GRANDMA** Frank Schaeffer **$14.95 (With 4 items) $8.97

The funniest novel ever written about growing up Protestant

PORTOFINO** Frank Schaeffer **$7.95 (With 4 items) $4.77

The best seller about being young, in love and a pastors child.

MUSIC CD

FIRST FRUIT CD $22.95 (With 4 items) $13.77

A fantastic CD of Byzantine chant in English.

VIDEO TAPES *Frank Schaeffer*

ORTHODOX EVANGELISM** 2VHS TAPES **$29.95 (With 4 items) $17.95

A great Video on how to spread the word about the Orthodox Church.

DEFENSE OF ORTHODOXY** 3 VHS TAPES **$59.85 (With 4 items) $35.91

The most widely used video series on Orthodoxy ever made.

TRUE STATE OF THE UNION** 1 VHS TAPE **$19.95 (With 4 items) $12.

The moral state of America from an Orthodox point of view. Abortion, the family other social issues.

JOURNEY TO ORTHODOXY** 1 VHS TAPE **$19.95 (With 4 items) $12.

How Frank Schaeffer converted to the Orthodox church. A personal journey.

CD ROM

MOUNT ATHOS CD ROM $45. (With 4 items) $27

The finest multi-media presentation of Orthodox monasticism.

FOR FASTEST SERVICE CALL TOLL FREE

800 636 2470 NON-USA CALL 978 462 7645 FAX 978 462 5079

***Order over the Web!* www.reginaorthodoxpress.com**

Regina Orthodox Press

40% OFF For Any 5 Items or More!

Check or Credit Card ***MUST*** *Be Enclosed*

CREDIT CARD, CHECK, WEB, MAIL, CALL OR FAX YOUR ORDER TODAY!

BOOKS

# Copies_______	*TWO PATHS*	*$22.95*
# Copies_______	*THE SCANDAL OF GENDER*	*$22.95*
# Copies_______	*ETERNAL DAY*	*$22.95*
# Copies_______	*THE FAITH*	*$22.95*
# Copies_______	*THE WAY*	*$22.95*
# Copies_______	*LETTERS TO Fr. ARISTOTLE*	*$22.95*
# Copies_______	*DANCING ALONE*	*$20.00*
# Copies_______	*PORTOFINO*	*$7.95*
# Copies_______	*SAVING GRANDM*	*$14.95*

VIDEO TAPES

# Copies_______	*DEFENSE OF ORTHODOXY*	*$59.95*
# Copies_______	*PERSONAL JOURNEY*	*$19.95*
# Copies_______	*ORTHODOX EVANGELISM*	*$29.95*
# Copies_______	*TRUE STATE OF THE UNION*	*$19.95*

MUSIC CD

# Copies_______	*FIRST FRUITS CD*	*22.95*

CD ROM

# Copies_______	*MOUNT ATHOS CD ROM*	*$45.00*

Subtotal $

40% DISCOUNT (ANY 5 ITEMS or MORE)	*$______*
Add 10% of total for shipping & handling	*$______*
*(Non U. S. add 20% shipping & handling!)_*	
MA residents add 5% sales tax	*$______*
GRAND TOTAL	*$______*

NAME____
ADDRESS_____________________________________
CITY____
STATE_______________________ZIP_____________
E-mail #____________________________________
Telephone___________________________________
MASTERCARD or VISA #_______________________Exp. Date
SIGNATURE___________________________________

FOR FASTEST SERVICE CALL TOLL FREE !

800 636 2470 *Non US 978 462 7645 FAX 978 462 5079*

Regina Orthodox Press PO Box 5288 Salisbury MA 01952

Order over the Web! **www.reginaorthodoxpress.com**